OHIO COURTS

Return to Bill Hamann
Dean of Legal Studies

Janis L. Walter, Esq.
Associate Professor of Legal Studies
University of Cincinnati

Pearson
Prentice Hall
Legal Series

PEARSON
Prentice
Hall

Upper Saddle River, New Jersey 07458

Library of Congress Cataloging-in-Publication Data

Walter, Janis L.
Ohio courts / Janis L. Walter.— 1st ed.
p. cm.
Includes bibliographical references and index.
ISBN 0-13-119923-4
1. Courts—Ohio. I. Title.
KFO510.W33 2006
347.771'01—dc22 2004026569

Director of Production and Manufacturing: Bruce Johnson
Consulting Editor: Enika Schulze and Nancy Blanchette/Athena Group, Inc.
Editorial Assistant: Cyrenne Bolt de Freitas
Marketing Manager: Leigh Ann Sims
Managing Editor—Production: Mary Carnis
Manufacturing Buyer: Ilene Sanford
Production Liaison: Denise Brown
Production Editor: Judy Ludowitz/Carlisle Publishers Services
Composition: Carlisle Communications, Ltd.
Design Director: Cheryl Asherman
Senior Design Coordinator/Cover Design: Christopher Weigand
Cover Image/Photographer: Ron Chapple/Taxi/Getty Images, Inc.
Cover Printer: Offset Paperback Manufacturers, Inc.
Printer/Binder: Offset Paperback Manufacturers, Inc.

Ohio Courts is designed as a textbook for classroom use. The information contained herein is intended only for educational and informational purposes.

Pearson Education Ltd.
Pearson Education Singapore Pte. Ltd.
Pearson Education Canada, Ltd.
Pearson Education—Japan
Pearson Education Australia Pty. Limited
Pearson Education North Asia Ltd.
Pearson Educación de Mexico, S. A. de C.V.
Pearson Education Malaysia Pte. Ltd.

PEARSON
Prentice Hall

10 9 8 7 6 5 4 3 2 1
ISBN 0-13-119923-4

CONTENTS

PREFACE

Ohio Courts has been written to aid the student in the study of law. It contains specific information and diagrams on the courts of Ohio—the court's jurisdiction, personnel connected with each court, and a brief discussion of procedural issues including the utilization of alternate dispute resolution methods and legal research sources.

The attached Appendices will challenge the student to perform legal research using case law and statutes, as well as guide them through various Web sites that contain a plethora of practical information.

Many individuals have contributed to and encouraged the writing of this book, and I would be remiss not to properly thank them. First, my deepest appreciation goes to the many paralegal students who I have had the honor of teaching at the University of Cincinnati. A special thanks goes to Robyn Shapiro for her never-ending assistance. Last, but never least, thanks go to my husband, Roger Wright, and my children, Emma and Peter.

It is my sincere hope that this book will contribute in some way to your study of the law!

Janis L. Walter

ABOUT THE AUTHOR

Janis L. Walter is an associate professor in the Criminal Justice Division at the University of Cincinnati. In addition to serving as paralegal program coordinator, she teaches a variety of legal courses, including domestic relations and civil litigation. Prior to teaching, she practiced civil and criminal law. She is licensed in the states of Ohio and Kentucky and still handles private adoptions. Ms. Walter currently resides in Cincinnati, Ohio with her husband, Roger Wright, and their children, Emma and Peter.

CHAPTER 1

1.1 Ohio Constitution

1.1.1 Introduction

Pursuant to the terms of the Northwest Ordinance, Ohio was required to submit a constitution before it could be considered for statehood. In November 1802, thirty-five delegates met at the constitutional convention to debate the numerous proposed provisions. The majority of those delegates were members of the Democratic-Republican Party who favored a weak central government. As expected, the first state constitution established a relatively weak executive branch, a strong legislative branch, and a judiciary to which judges were appointed by the legislature.

In 1850, the people of Ohio voted to hold a second constitutional convention. Unhappy with the strength of the legislature, an inadequate judicial system, and tax issues, a second constitution was adopted in 1851. The new constitution limited the legislators' powers and required the executive officers and judges to be elected by popular vote.

In response to additional problems that arose over the years, two more constitutional conventions were held that resulted in amendments. In 1873, at the third constitutional convention, the governor of Ohio was granted veto power. The fourth and final convention was held in 1912, where amendments were passed to help equalize the branches of government. Therefore, the 1851 constitution has been amended two times but has never been totally replaced.

The Ohio Constitution is organized into a Preamble and seventeen numbered articles that include the Bill of Rights and the framework of the government. Article II vests legislative power in a General Assembly that consists of the Senate and a House of Representatives.[1] A new legislative session is assembled every two years on the first Monday in January of the odd-numbered years. However, since there is no limit on the days the General Assembly may convene, it can respond immediately to emergency situations. Article III vests the executive power in the governor, lieutenant governor, secretary of state, attorney general, treasurer, and auditor.[2] It declares the governor as having the supreme executive power.[3] The governor is limited to two consecutive four-year terms.[4]

Article IV outlines the court system in Ohio. It vests the judicial power of the state in a supreme court, courts of appeals, courts of common pleas and divisions thereof, and such other courts inferior to the supreme court as may from time to time be established by law.[5] Those inferior courts established by statute include municipal, county, court of claims, mayors, and small claims.

Whenever two-thirds of the members elected to each branch of the General Assembly decide that it is necessary to call for a convention, to revise, amend, or change the constitution, they shall make a recommendation to the electors.[6] The electors shall vote on the issue and, assuming that they find a convention necessary, shall select candidates for the constitutional convention.[7]

Either branch of the General Assembly may propose amendments to the Ohio Constitution.[8] If three-fifths of the members of Ohio General Assembly support the amendment, it will be placed on a separate ballot without party designation of any kind for the Ohio voters to vote upon it.[9]

1.1.2 Interplay among the Three Branches

The three branches of Ohio government, the legislative, executive, and judicial, divide the powers of the state government between them. This creates "checks and balances" between the three branches that precludes a branch from becoming too powerful. The Ohio legislature is responsible for creating and enacting laws known as statutes, but the judiciary has the right to interpret those statutes through deciding cases brought before them. The executive branch determines if the statute should be executed. If the courts determine that a statute violates the United States Constitution or Ohio Constitution, they can strike it down by declaring it unconstitutional. Such decisions may be published and are referred to as case law or common law. Courts and attorneys rely upon such case law in areas not covered by statutes and for use as precedents. Precedents advocate that the point of law should be followed when similar or identical facts are before the court, thereby giving citizens a reasonable expectation as to an outcome.

In addition to the three branches of government, Ohio has established administrative agencies to handle a large and diverse number of issues. Administrative agencies are able to respond to issues more quickly than Ohio General Assembly, and they possess expertise in their particular area. Agencies pass rules and regulations that have the force and effect of statutes; they can require or prohibit certain actions and may impose penalties for violations. Laws passed by administrative agencies can be found in the **Ohio Administrative Code.**

CHAPTER 2

2.1 State Courts

2.1.1 Relationship to Federal Courts

In addition to the state courts, Ohio has two United States District Courts located within its boundaries. The Ohio courts focus on issues concerning Ohio law and its constitution. The federal courts deal with matters involving federal questions, that is, federal statutes, the U.S. Constitution, and treaties. Federal courts also have subject matter jurisdiction over cases involving diversity of citizenship. Diversity jurisdiction allows a plaintiff from one state to sue a defendant from another state in federal district court if the amount in controversy exceeds $75,000, exclusive of costs and interest. In diversity cases, the state and federal courts have concurrent jurisdiction. Therefore, a plaintiff must select between state or federal court. When both courts have jurisdiction and the plaintiff elects to initiate his claim in state court, the defendant has the option of removing the case from the state court to the federal court by exercising **removal jurisdiction.** If this option was chosen, the federal courts would apply state law to the case.

The trial court of the federal system is the United States District Court. There are two district courts in Ohio, the Northern and Southern. Each district is divided into two divisions, the eastern and western.

- The United States District Court for the Northern District of Ohio, Eastern Division has divisional offices in Akron, Cleveland, and Youngstown.
- The United States District Court of the Northern District of Ohio, Western Division has a divisional office in Toledo.
- The United States District Court of the Southern District of Ohio, Eastern Division is located in Columbus.
- The United States District Court of the Southern District of Ohio, Western Division holds court in Cincinnati and Dayton.

If a party is dissatisfied with a decision of the federal trial court, they may appeal to the federal court of appeals. The federal court of appeals is divided into thirteen circuits. The federal court of appeals with jurisdiction in Ohio is the United States Court of Appeals for the Sixth Circuit. It is located in Cincinnati and includes Ohio, Kentucky, Tennessee, and Michigan. The Sixth Circuit will hear any appeal from a district court located in one of these states since it has **mandatory appellate jurisdiction.** Appeals from the United States Court of Appeals for the Sixth Circuit, any of the other circuits, or the Ohio Supreme Court may proceed to the United States Supreme Court. The majority of the cases that reach the U.S. Supreme Court fall within that court's **discretionary appellate jurisdiction.** An aggrieved party may file a petition

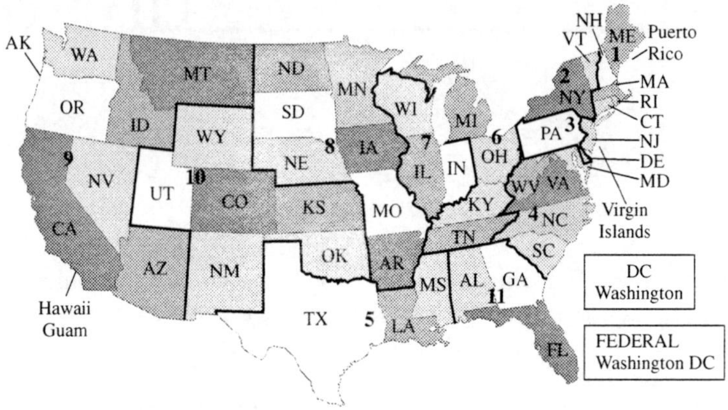

Diagram 1 The Thirteen Federal Judicial Circuits

for **writ of certiorari** requesting that the court accept their appeal. The court will grant certiorari review in only a small number of cases.

2.1.2 Televising Court Proceedings

Pursuant to the **Rules of Superintendence for the Courts of Ohio,** a written request can be made to allow broadcasting in court proceedings that are open to the public as provided by Ohio law.[10] It is within the presiding judge's discretion whether to permit the broadcasting. Once ordered, the judge may consult with the media in order to determine where the operators and equipment should be positioned in the courtroom. The judge may prohibit any arrangement that imposes on the judge or court personnel or distracts from the proceedings.[11] At no time can there be any audio pickup or a broadcast of conferences that would violate the attorney-client privilege, conversations between cocounsel, or conferences conducted at the bench between counsel and the judge.[12] Any violation of the judge's conditions or those prescribed by the rules will result in a revocation of the permission to broadcast the trial or hearing.[13]

2.1.3 State Attorney

The chief legal officer for the state of Ohio is the Ohio Attorney General. He serves as legal counsel to the governor, other statewide elected officials, the Ohio General Assembly, and all state departments, agencies, boards, and commissions. Upon request from other elected officials and county prosecutors, he issues formal legal opinions. The issues handled by the Attorney General's office may range from consumer fraud and criminal justice to environmental enforcement and constitutional challenges.

Each county has a prosecuting attorney who is elected by the residents of the county for a four-year term. As prosecuting attorney, he is responsible for both civil and criminal cases within the county. He has the authority to investigate and prosecute crimes and to appear before, present evidence, and give legal advise to the Grand Jury. The county attorney is also the chief legal advisor to all county boards and officers, township boards and officers, public libraries, and local school districts. Therefore, if a local officer is sued, the county attorney will represent them.

2.1.4 Public Defenders

The Ohio statutes created a public defender commission to provide, supervise, and coordinate legal representation at state expense for **indigents** (people who cannot afford attorneys) and other persons.[14] The commission consists of nine members. Of those members, one is designated as chairperson and appointed by the governor with the advice and consent of the senate. The chairperson must be an attorney admitted to the practice of law in Ohio. Of the remaining eight members, the governor and Supreme Court each appoint four members. Two of the four appointees must be licensed attorneys in Ohio.[15]

Among many other responsibilities, the commission is required to appoint a state public defender that is a licensed attorney with at least four years of law practice experience in the state of Ohio.[16] The state public defender and his assistants may provide legal representation in all courts throughout the state to indigent adults and juveniles who are charged with a crime that may result in imprisonment.[17] They will also represent an incarcerated person who claims they are unlawfully imprisoned or detained and indigents in parole and probation revocation matters.[18]

In addition to the state public defender's office, the statutes allow for the county commissioners to establish a county public defenders office.[19] If a county system is created, the state public defenders office is not required to represent indigent clients in that county.[20] The county public defenders are responsible to provide legal representation for indigents in both felony and misdemeanor criminal cases in their respective county. Staff attorneys represent misdemeanants in Municipal Court, criminally accused adults and juveniles in Juvenile Court, and nonsupport defendants in Juvenile and Domestic Relations Court. Representation is limited to those criminal, traffic, or delinquency charges that carry the possibility of incarceration if convicted. In counties that have established drug courts, staff attorneys may be assigned full-time to the court. Although the drug courts are considered nonadversarial, the attorneys assist the clients at every stage of the process, advising them of the legal ramifications, thereby enabling them to make informed decisions.

The county public defenders office may also maintain a list of private attorneys who have agreed to handle more serious felony cases, Juvenile Court dependency proceedings, and paternity cases.[21] The assigned attorneys are rotated to ensure that cases are equally distributed. They represent the client through trial level and into any necessary postconviction proceedings, including motions and appeals.

If the county chooses not to establish a county system, the county commissioners of any county may adopt a resolution to establish a nonprofit corporation or pay counsel who are either personally selected by the indigent person or appointed by the court.[22] Assigned and court-appointed attorneys accept cases on a reduced fee basis pursuant to established rates.

2.1.5 Court Rules

Specific rules or laws govern every phase of civil and criminal litigation. These laws are divided into two major categories: substantive and procedural law. Substantive law defines the rights and obligations of an individual. The legal elements of a crime or tort are examples of substantive law. There are several sources of substantive law, but the most common are statutes, court decisions, and administrative regulations. Procedural laws set the rules and methods employed to obtain one's rights. The steps required to annul a marriage, how to request a jury trial, and how long one has to file a claim are examples of procedural law.

Attorneys must process a claim pursuant to the applicable rules since failure to do so could result in a dismissal of the case. To guide them, the Ohio Supreme Court has promulgated rules that govern the practice and procedure in all courts of the state.[23] However, the Ohio Constitution limits this power by prohibiting the Ohio Supreme Court from prescribing procedural laws that abridge, enlarge, or modify any substantive right.[24] The Ohio Supreme Court also allows other courts to adopt additional rules concerning local practice in their respective courts that are not inconsistent with the rules promulgated by the Ohio Supreme Court.[25] Therefore, there are several sets of rules that an attorney must consult before proceeding.

Rules applicable to a civil trial can be found in the **Ohio Rules of Civil Procedure.** Likewise, the **Ohio Rules of Criminal Procedure** governs a criminal trial. The *Ohio Rules of Civil Procedure* contain the rules on how to handle a civil case, beginning with the drafting of the complaint and service of process through discovery, trial, judgment and posttrial motions. The *Ohio Rules of Civil Procedure* contain simplistic forms like sample summons, complaints, motions, and judgments.

The Ohio Supreme Court has authorized each county to adopt local rules of practice that facilitate the expeditious disposition of both civil and criminal cases within that particular county, while at the same time safeguarding the rights of the litigants. As previously stated, the local rules cannot be inconsistent with rules promulgated by the Ohio Supreme Court.[26] Generally, the local rules add or modify the statewide rules. Therefore, each county has adopted **Local Rules of Practice of the Court of Common Pleas** that affect the general division of the court of common pleas. Each division may also adopt local rules such as the **Local Rules and Guidelines for the Court of Domestic Relations** and **Rules of the Probate Division.** There are also **Local Rules of Practice of the Court of Claims of Ohio.** The local rules may address such issues as the term and hours of the court, the duty of the judges, information regarding juries and jury selection, arbitration, and requirements for pleadings. For example, Hamilton County local rules require pleadings to be typewritten or printed on 8½ by 11 inch, unfolded, bond paper.[27]

The Supreme Court of Ohio has also adopted **Rules of Superintendence for the Courts of Ohio** pursuant to the authority granted them in the Ohio Constitution.[28] These rules are applicable to all courts of appeals, courts of common pleas, municipal courts, and county courts in the state.[29] Like the other rules, their purpose is to ensure the prompt disposition of cases. They discuss issues including the selection, term, powers, and duties of presiding judges and administrative judges, the use of attorney registration numbers, security plans, notifying law enforcement agencies of criminal and civil protection orders, and court appointments.

The **Ohio Rules of Criminal Procedure** guide a case, except those classified as traffic cases, through the criminal process beginning with the arrest, initial appearance, and preliminary hearing and moving through the discovery, trial, and posttrial matters to sentencing. The criminal rules also contain useful sample forms. Each county's local rules may also contain sections applicable to the practice and procedure involved in criminal cases. They may describe the procedures required for courthouse security, HIV testing, bail, and the issuance of warrants for probation violation. The **Ohio Traffic Rules** prescribe the rules to be followed in all Ohio courts for traffic cases.[30] The Supreme Court promulgates the traffic rules pursuant to their authority granted in the **Ohio Revised Code.**[31] Their purpose is to secure a fair, impartial, and speedy trial in traffic cases without unjustifiable expense.[32]

The **Ohio Rules of Evidence** apply to all trials except for those held in Small Claims.[33] The rules do not apply to arbitration or contempt hearings, proceedings before the grand juries, or special nonadversary statutory proceedings.[34] The purpose of the rules of evidence is to provide procedures for the adjudication of causes to ensure that truth may be ascertained and proceedings justly determined.[35] They govern the admissibility of evidence and competency of witnesses to testify. Evidence should be relevant and reliable, but not prejudicial, misleading, or confusing.[36] The *Ohio Rules of Evidence* declare some conversations as privileged, which means that they are not admissible during a trial. However, the rules defer to the Ohio statutes and principles of common law on this issue.[37]

The **Ohio Rules of Juvenile Procedure** prescribe the procedure to be followed in all juvenile courts in Ohio except for appeals to review any judgment, order, or ruling, trials of criminal actions, paternity cases, or the commitment of mentally ill or mentally retarded.[38] Their stated purpose is to ensure the just determination of every juvenile court proceeding by providing the parties with a fair hearing.[39]

Civil and criminal cases appealed to the Courts of Appeals from trial courts, the tax board, and juvenile court are governed by the **Ohio Rules of Appellate Procedure.**[40] The rules guide an appeal beginning with the filing of the Notice of Appeal and docketing statement through the filing and service of briefs and oral arguments. They provide the details for form of briefs, including **amicus curiae** or "friend of the court" briefs. An individual or group, not a party to the action, who has an interest in the outcome of the litigation may file an amicus curiae brief. The amicus curiae brief provides the court with additional information to assist them in reaching a decision. For example, in a decision regarding abortion rights, Planned Parenthood and Right to Life organizations may wish to file amicus curiae briefs. An amicus curiae brief may be filed with written consent of all parties or by leave of court.[41] The rules also provide guidelines for oral arguments including content, requirements for appearance, and length of time. Attorneys need to be extremely careful because each appellate district has also adopted their own rules that may modify or supplement the *Ohio Rules of Appellate Procedure.* These rules are known as **Supplemental Local Appellate Rules.** Although these rules cannot be inconsistent with the state rules, they often add requirements to the appeals that can result in dismissal if not followed. For example, the First Appellate District recently added a requirement that all briefs secured with staples must be covered to ensure that the staples do not protrude from the back of the brief. If the brief is submitted with an uncovered staple, it is subject to being stricken.[42]

Cases that are appealed to the Ohio Supreme Court or ones over which the court has original jurisdiction (quo warranto, mandamus, habeas corpus, prohibition, and procedendo) are controlled by the **Rules of Practice of the Supreme Court of Ohio.** In order to practice before the Ohio Supreme Court, attorneys must either be registered for active status with the Clerk of the Supreme Court or have complied with the **pro hac vice** requirements. At times, the Ohio Supreme Court will permit an out-of-state attorney not licensed to practice in Ohio to appear before the court to handle a specific case. This is referred to as being admitted pro hac vice. The attorney is admitted temporarily for the duration of the case and must be assisted by an Ohio licensed attorney.[43] Attorneys involved in death penalty appeals before the Ohio Supreme Court must be additionally certified.[44] The rules govern the appeal from the Notice of Appeal and Memorandum in Support of Jurisdiction to the briefs and oral arguments. There are special requirements applicable to death penalty cases.[45] These rules state that original actions filed before the Ohio Supreme Court should follow the *Ohio Rules of Civil Procedure* unless clearly inapplicable.[46] To further assist the attorney, the Ohio Supreme Court has added sample forms including Notices of Appeal, Memorandums in Support of Jurisdiction, briefs, and a praecipe to the court reporter in a capital case. The Supreme Court has also established **Administrative Rules of the Supreme Court of Ohio** that includes a records retention schedule and **Supreme Court Rules for the Reporting of Opinions** that governs the reporting of Supreme Court, Courts of Appeals, and inferior court decisions.

2.1.6 Juries

There are two types of juries in the state of Ohio—**grand juries** and **petit juries.** Each has a unique function in the system. The grand jury is used exclusively in criminal cases, and the petit jury is used for trials. The grand jury secretly hears testimony presented to it by a prosecutor to determine whether an indictment should be returned. If the grand jury decides that there is probable cause that a crime has been committed and the defendant is the one who committed that crime, they return an indictment. An **indictment** is the formal criminal charge issued by the grand jury stating they found sufficient evidence that the defendant committed a crime and should stand trial. Grand jury proceedings are **ex parte** proceedings—they take place outside of the presence of the defendant and his counsel. In fact, in addition to the grand jury members, only the prosecutor, stenographer, and witness under examination are present while the grand jury is deliberating or voting.[47]

Felonies that are punishable by death or life imprisonment must be prosecuted by indictment in Ohio.[48] However, other felonies may proceed on an **information,** as opposed to the indictment.[49] An information is a formal accusation made by a prosecuting attorney, not a grand jury.

The grand jury consists of nine members, including a foreperson, plus not more than five alternates.[50] The rules require that an indictment may be returned only upon the concurrence of seven or more jurors.[51] A grand jury usually serves for four months but can be required by the prosecutor to serve up to nine months.[52]

Unlike the grand jury, which determines whether a defendant should be charged with a felony, a petit jury tries civil and criminal cases. A petit jury is a group of citizens who hear the evidence presented by both sides at trial and determine the facts in dispute. "Petit" is French for "small," thus distinguishing the petit jury from the grand jury, which traditionally consisted of larger numbers of jurors. The grand jury must only have probable cause to issue an indictment, but this standard is not applicable to petit jurors. The burden of proof in a criminal case is **beyond a reasonable doubt.** In most civil cases, the jury must determine by a preponderance of the evidence that the defendant violated the plaintiff's rights. A **preponderance of the evidence** means that more of the evidence favors the plaintiff's position than the opposing side. In a minority of civil cases, the burden is **clear and convincing evidence,** which means that it is very probable that the defendant violated the plaintiff's rights. This standard requires a higher degree of proof than preponderance of the evidence.

The number of jurors on a petit jury varies depending on the type of case. In criminal felony cases, a defendant is entitled to a jury consisting of twelve members.[53] In misdemeanor cases, juries shall consist of eight.[54] If the defendant is jointly charged with a felony and misdemeanor, the jury shall consist of twelve members.[55] All criminal cases require the jurors to return a unanimous verdict.[56] In most civil cases, the jury shall be composed of eight members unless the jury demand specifies a lesser number.[57] An exception involves an action for appropriation of a right of way brought by a corporation pursuant to Article XIII, Section 5, of the Ohio Constitution. In such cases, the jury shall be composed of twelve members unless the demand specifies a lesser number.[58] Civil cases require three-fourths of the jury to agree upon the verdict. Therefore, if the jury consists of eight members, six members must be in agreement for a verdict.[59] When the requisite number of jurors cannot agree on a verdict, the jury is referred to as a **hung jury.** In those situations, the case may be retried, but it will be tried to a new jury.

The state of Ohio considers jury duty an obligation of all qualified citizens. The state statutes allow potential jurors to be randomly summoned from the list of registered voters and licensed drivers.[60] However, they also authorize each county to adopt local rules regarding jury selection.[61] Many counties have opted to only select jurors from the registered voters list since they believe that this list is representative and inclusive of the adult population of their particular county. In addition to being a registered voter or licensed driver, a person is eligible for jury duty if they are eighteen years or older, a citizen of the United States, a resident of the jurisdiction in which they have been summoned to serve, able to communicate in the English language, and have not been convicted of a felony.[62] The opportunity for jury service shall not be denied or limited on the basis of race, national origin, gender, age, religious belief, income, occupation, disability, or any other factor that discriminates against a cognizable group.[63] Prospective jurors may be exempt from service for several reasons, including the following:

- They are over 70 years of age and request to be excused.
- Service would cause financial, childcare, or school hardship.
- They are members of certain professions, that is, firemen, physicians, and lawyers.

Jurors may also defer their service for a reasonably short period of time with the permission of the judge or a specifically authorized court official, usually a jury commissioner.

The jury commissioners of each county estimate the approximate number of jurors needed for the following jury year and then randomly select the list. Potential jurors are notified of their service by ordinary mail. Generally their term of service is three weeks. A panel of jurors (known as **veniremen**) is selected for a particular courtroom. The judge will swear in the panel and briefly explain the nature of the case. The attorneys and/or the judge will conduct a questioning process known as **voir dire examination.**[64] A venireman may be excused from duty if he knows any of the parties, witnesses, attorneys, or judge. He may also be excused if he is familiar with the facts of the case, has an interest in the outcome, has already formed an opinion about the case, or has a bias or prejudice that would affect the outcome. These grounds for disqualifying a juror are known as **challenges for cause.** In criminal cases, a juror may also be challenged for cause if the juror is a chronic alcoholic or drug dependent.[65] Each side has an unlimited number of challenges for cause. Each party may also **peremptorily challenge** three jurors in a civil case, which is a challenge for any reason, absent discrimination.[66] In criminal felony cases, each party receives four challenges, which increases to six challenges in capital cases.[67] Members of the panel who are accepted by both sides become jurors who determine the outcome of the case.

2.1.7 Judges

The **Code of Judicial Conduct** establishes standards and discipline for the ethical conduct of judges and provides guidance to candidates for judicial office. The *Code of Judicial Conduct* applies to judges and justices, whether full-time, part-time, **pro tempore** (temporary judge), or a retired judge recalled to service. It also applies to referees, special masters, court commissioners, and magistrates. The *Code of Judicial Conduct* consists of seven canons, two of which are currently reserved, that are broad statements about conduct. Each canon is subdivided into rules that more specifically define the canon. The canons and the divisions are authoritative but should not impinge on the judge's independence in rendering decisions. The five canons outlining the ethical obligations of Ohio judges are as follows:

1. A Judge Should Uphold the Integrity and Independence of the Judiciary.
2. A Judge Shall Respect and Comply with the Law and Shall Act at all Times in a Manner That Promotes Public Confidence in the Integrity and Impartiality of the Judiciary.
3. A Judge Shall Perform the Duties of Judicial Office Impartially and Diligently.
4. A Judge Shall Avoid Impropriety and the Appearance of Impropriety in all of the Judge's Activities.
5. Judges and Judicial Candidates Should Refrain from Political Activity Inappropriate to Judicial Office.

Failure to comply with the canons or rules may result in disciplinary action against the judge. However, the *Code of Judicial Conduct* is not designed as a basis for civil liability or criminal prosecution, nor can it be invoked by lawyers for a tactical advantage in a proceeding.

Full-time judges are required to complete forty hours of continuing judicial education every two years.[68]

2.1.8 Attorneys

The Ohio Supreme Court governs the admission of attorneys to the practice of law in the state of Ohio. To be admitted, an applicant must be at least 21 years of age, have earned a bachelor's degree from an accredited college or university and a J.D. or L.L.B. degree from an American Bar Association approved law school, demonstrate the requisite character, fitness, and moral qualifications, and pass both the Ohio bar examination and the Multistate Professional Responsibility Examination. Having met these requirements, the applicant must take the oath of office affirming to support the Constitutions and laws of the United States and Ohio and abide by the **Code of Professional Responsibility.** Attorneys are declared "officers of the court" and are expected to conduct themselves with dignity and civility and show respect toward judges, court staff, clients, fellow professionals, and all other persons.

Attorneys must register with the Ohio Supreme Court and be issued an attorney registration number to be entitled to practice in Ohio. There is no mandatory requirement that an attorney be a member of the Ohio Bar Association, although there are advantages to membership. Any attorney practicing in Ohio is subject to the **Supreme Court Rules for the Government of the Bar.**

These rules, as well as the oath of office, bind all attorneys to the *Code of Professional Responsibility*. The *Code of Professional Responsibility* governs issues such as maintaining the integrity and competence of the legal profession, the attorney's duty to the client, and the necessity of avoiding even the appearance of professional impropriety. The willful breach of the *Code of Professional Responsibility* will result in punishment by reprimand, suspension, disbarment, or probation. All grievances involving alleged attorney misconduct are handled through the Board of Commissioners of Grievances and Discipline of the Supreme Court, who make a recommendation to the Ohio Supreme Court. Once the Ohio Supreme Court has finalized the sanction, the disciplinary order, or acceptance of a resignation from the practice of law, it shall be published in the *Ohio Official Reports,* the *Ohio State Bar Association Report,* a local bar association publication, if any, and the newspaper of general circulation in the county designated by the Board of Commissioners.

To maintain and improve the quality of legal services in Ohio, the Ohio Supreme Court requires continuing legal education for Ohio attorneys. Each attorney authorized to practice law in Ohio shall complete at least twenty-four credit hours every two years. Of those twenty-four hours, thirty minutes of instruction shall be on substance abuse, sixty minutes related to the *Code of Professional Responsibility,* and sixty minutes related to professionalism. Any attorney who fails to satisfy the applicable minimum continuing legal education requirements may be subject to sanctions that could include a fee, a public reprimand, probation, or suspension from the practice of law.

The Ohio Supreme Court allows attorneys to declare themselves as specialists in certain areas of practice. The purpose of this rule is to enhance public access to appropriate legal services by regulating the certification of lawyers as specialists. To be considered for specialist status, an attorney must be registered as an active member of the bar for at least three years and be certified by an agency approved by the **Commission on Certification of Attorneys as Specialist.** The certification verifies that the attorney has demonstrated an enhanced level of skill and expertise as well as substantial involvement in the specialty area. They may be required to pass a written test and submit evidence that they have completed additional continuing legal education requirements, taught the subject, participated as a speaker, panelist, or workshop leader, or written a book on the subject matter. Once certified, the specialist must complete twelve hours of continuing legal education every two years in each certified specialty area. Some of the recognized areas of law subject to specialization designation are as follows: (1) Estate Planning, Trust, and Probate Law, (2) Federal Taxation Law, (3) Elder Law, (4) Business, Commercial, and Industrial Real Property Law, and (5) Residential Real Property Law.

Rule VIII of the *Supreme Court Rules for the Government of the Bar* requires the establishment of a Clients' Security Fund of Ohio to be funded by the Attorney Registration Fund. The purpose of the fund is to aid in ameliorating the losses caused to clients and others by dishonest members of the bar acting as an attorney or fiduciary. The claimant may submit a claim to the **Board**

of Commissioners of the Clients' Security Fund of Ohio, who may grant awards not to exceed fifty thousand dollars.

2.1.9 Legal Assistants and Paralegals

Legal assistant and paralegal are terms that apply to a person who performs legal duties under the supervision of an attorney. In the past, these terms have been used interchangeably; however, that trend is fading. Today, many legal secretaries refer to themselves as "legal assistants," while the term "paralegal" is being used exclusively for those who perform actual legal functions with the exception of giving legal advice and trying cases. Many academic programs and associations have recently changed their name to reflect this trend and eliminate confusion. In 2003, the American Bar Association's Standing Committee on Legal Assistants modified their name. The new name is the Standing Committee on Paralegals. Ohio has no provision to license or regulate paralegals; therefore, paralegals may not provide legal services without the supervision of an attorney. There are also no specific requirements to become a paralegal; however, the most widely recognized manner is to complete an academic degree from a program approved by the American Bar Association. Paralegals may obtain an associate or bachelor's degree or complete a postbaccalaureate certificate in paralegal studies. Paralegals may also receive on-the-job training.

There are three widely recognized national paralegal associations—the National Association of Legal Assistants (NALA), the National Federal of Paralegal Associations, and the American Alliance of Paralegals, Inc. (AAPI), all of which are dedicated to the advancement of the paralegal profession. NALA sponsors a voluntary examination for paralegals that, if successfully passed, allows a paralegal to become certified in a specific area of practice. This certification may assist the paralegal in obtaining employment or receiving a promotion.

2.1.10 Unauthorized Practice of Law

The Ohio Supreme Court Rules prohibit the rendering of legal services for another by any person not admitted to practice in Ohio. The purpose of this rule is to protect the unsuspecting public from obtaining legal services from an unqualified individual with no legal training. Although the lure of cheaper fees may be appealing, the consequences may be devastating. If an attorney commits an error that results in malpractice, the client has some protection through a civil lawsuit and attorney discipline. Most attorneys also carry malpractice insurance that would cover any monetary losses. However, nonattorneys engaged in the unauthorized practice of law offer no such relief to an aggrieved client.

Upon the filing of a complaint, the **Board of Commissioners on the Unauthorized Practice of Law of the Supreme Court** will determine by a preponderance of the evidence whether the respondent has engaged in the unauthorized practice of law. They submit their findings and recommendations for review to the Ohio Supreme Court. If the Court concurs with the Board's findings, they will issue an order prohibiting the respondent from engaging in any such conduct in the future and may order the respondent to pay the Board and claimant's costs and expenses. The order shall be published in the *Ohio Official Reports,* the *Ohio State Bar Association Report,* the local bar association publication, if any, and the local newspaper of the largest general circulation, all at the cost of the respondent. The respondent may also be subject to criminal misdemeanor prosecution for the unauthorized practice of law.[69]

CHAPTER 3

3.1 Ohio Court System

3.1.1 Trial and Appellate Courts

The Ohio court system is comprised of several courts: Ohio Supreme Court, Ohio Courts of Appeals, Courts of Common Pleas, Municipal Courts, County Courts, Mayors' Courts, and the Court of Claims. The courts of common pleas, municipal courts, and county courts hear both civil and criminal trials. As a result of the large number of cases in a particular area, some counties have subdivided their courts of common pleas into divisions that hear a particular subject. For example, there are domestic relations, probate, and juvenile divisions. Small Claims Court is a division of municipal court or county court. There is no separate traffic court in Ohio.

The Supreme Court and Courts of Appeals have mainly appellate jurisdiction; however, in limited circumstances, they have original jurisdiction. Most of the trials occur in the common pleas, municipal, or county courts. Trials can be held before a jury, if properly requested, or before the judge. When a case is tried by a judge, this is referred to as a **bench trial.** A plaintiff must commence their case in one of the trial courts that have **subject matter jurisdiction,** meaning that the court has the authority to hear that particular type of case. One area that the municipal court has subject matter jurisdiction over is civil actions where the amount in controversy is less than $15,000. Therefore, a plaintiff could file a breach of contract action or a tort action in municipal court if they are seeking less than $15,000 in damages from the defendant. Once there is a verdict, the losing party may appeal the case to the next highest appellate court. For example, if the losing party in municipal court wishes to appeal, the case would be heard by the Court of Appeals. The common pleas court could not hear the appeal since they do not have appellate jurisdiction except for in some administrative decisions.

To be successful on appeal, the appellant must show that a harmful error of law was committed. The appellate courts will not review questions of fact decided by the jury or judge. If the appellate court concurs with the appellant's contention that a harmful error was made by the trial court, they may reverse the decision. If they find that there was no harmful error, the appellant may have the option of pursuing another appeal before the Ohio Supreme Court. However, because appeals are expensive and the likelihood of being successful decreases with each court, many times appellants choose not to appeal. In that case, the decision of the last court stands.

3.1.2 Criminal and Civil Cases

Cases brought before the court fall into two categories: **civil** and **criminal.** If there is a possibility of imprisonment, the case is classified as criminal. If there is no possibility of imprisonment, the case is considered as civil.

Crimes are further divided into two areas: **felonies** and **misdemeanors.** If the possibility of imprisonment is one year or more or death, the crime is a felony. An offense that carries a maximum penalty of less than one year is classified as a misdemeanor. Currently in Ohio, the longest sentence possible on a misdemeanor is six months. However, that is not true in other states since misdemeanors may be punishable for up to one year. Felonies and misdemeanors are classified depending on their severity and divided into degrees.

The Ohio Constitution guarantees a criminal defendant to a "speedy" trial. Generally, misdemeanors must be brought to trial within ninety days after the arrest, and felonies must be brought to trial within 270 days if the defendant is free on bail. If the defendant is incarcerated, each day counts as three days.

Civil cases usually involve claims for money from the defendant for their harmful acts to the plaintiff. Civil cases mainly fall into two categories—**contracts** and **torts.** Contract actions are when two or more parties make a legally binding agreement and one of the parties fails to fulfill their obligation. The nonbreaching party is entitled to a remedy, usually monetary damages. A tort is a civil action, other than a breach of contract, where the injured party may be entitled to compensation from the wrongdoer. Examples of some tort actions are negligence, product liability, malpractice, assault, trespass, and defamation. Other civil actions include divorce, dissolution, adoption, eviction, and name change.

In some civil cases, the plaintiff may be seeking a remedy other than monetary damages. These remedies are known as **equitable remedies** and include **injunctions** and **specific performance.** An injunction is a court order either prohibiting or requiring some action by the defendant. It is designed to prevent "irreparable harm" to the plaintiff. If the defendant is pumping chemicals into the plaintiff's pond, the plaintiff may obtain an injunction requiring the defendant to stop immediately. Specific performance is used in cases involving the sale of real estate or other unique property. When two parties have entered into a written contract for the sale of real estate and thereafter one of the parties refuses to perform the terms of the contract, the court will order "specific performance." Therefore, if the seller changed his mind and refused to sell the property, the court could order "specific performance" of the terms of the contract, requiring the owner to sell the real estate to the buyer.

There can be two actions arising from the same set of facts—one criminal resulting in the defendant's imprisonment and one civil where the plaintiff collects monetary damages from the defendant. For example, if a defendant is driving under the influence of intoxicants and causes an accident injuring the plaintiff, the defendant can be prosecuted for his criminal actions and the plaintiff can sue for monetary damages. Generally, the prosecutor determines whether a criminal prosecution will proceed, and the plaintiff, usually with the advise of retained legal counsel, will determine whether to proceed with a civil claim.

3.1.3 Venue

Venue is the geographically convenient location of the court where a case should be filed. There are eighty-eight counties in Ohio that may have subject matter jurisdiction (i.e., the Court of Common Pleas in each county has subject matter jurisdiction over civil actions greater than $15,000); however, the plaintiff must determine which of those eighty-eight counties would have proper venue in a civil case.

Venue of a Civil Case

Rule 3 the *Ohio Rules of Civil Procedure* governs venue in civil cases. The rule determines in which county a plaintiff may file their claim if the action was commenced in the state of Ohio. The rule provides as follows:

1. The county in which the defendant resides;
2. The county in which the defendant has his or her principal place of business;
3. A county in which the defendant conducted activity which gave rise to the claim for relief;
4. A county in which a public officer maintains his or her principal office if suit is brought against the officer in the officer's official capacity;
5. A county in which the property, or any part of the property, is situated if the subject of the action is real property or tangible personal property;
6. The county in which all or part of the claim for relief arose; or if the claim for relief arose upon a river, other watercourse, or a road, that is the boundary of the state, or of two or more counties, in any county bordering on the river, watercourse, or road, and opposite to the place where the claim for relief arose;
7. In actions described in Civ. R. 4.3 (out-of-state defendants), in the county where plaintiff resides;
8. In an action against an executor, administrator, guardian, or trustee, in the county in which they were appointed;
9. In actions for divorce, annulment, or legal separation, in the county in which the plaintiff is and has been a resident for at least ninety days immediately preceding the filing of the complaint;
10. In actions for a civil protection order, in the county in which the petitioner currently or temporarily resides;
11. If there is no available forum in the preceding sections, where the plaintiff resides, has his or her principal place of business, or regularly and systematically conducts business activity;
12. If there is no available forum in sections 1 through 11, the county in which the defendant has property or debts owing to the defendant

subject to attachment or garnishment or in a county in which the defendant has appointed an agent to receive service of process or in which an agent has been appointed by operation of law.

If an action has been filed in a county other than one stated to be proper under Rule 3 or where it appears that a defendant cannot receive a fair and impartial trial in the county where the claim was filed, the court or defense may ask that the case be transferred to another county. This request is known as a **change of venue.** If the claim was improperly filed pursuant to the terms of the rule, the court will move the case to a proper county. If the change is based on the defendant's inability to receive a fair and impartial trial, the case must be transferred to a county that adjoins the county where the action was originally commenced.[70]

Venue of a Criminal Case

Venue in a criminal case is proper in the county where the crime was committed. The venue of the case may be changed when it appears that a fair and impartial trial cannot be held in the court in which the action is pending.[71] The parties or the court can raise this issue. Unlike civil cases, a criminal case can be transferred to any court having jurisdiction of the subject matter outside the county where the trial would originally have been held.[72]

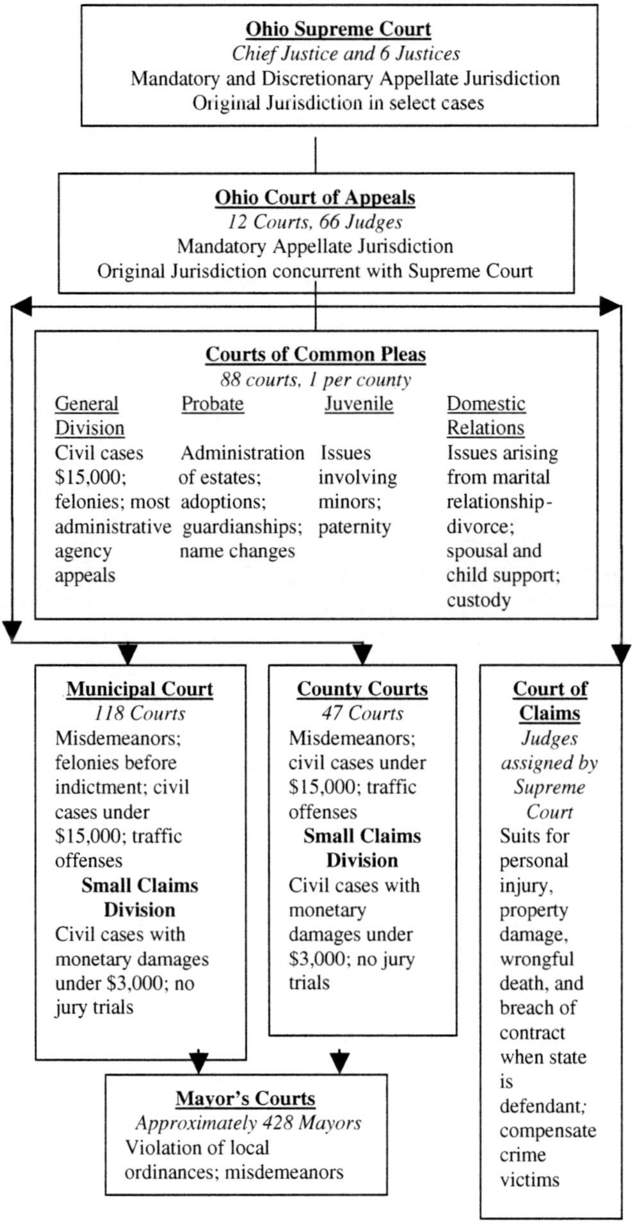

Diagram 2 The Ohio Court System

CHAPTER 4

4.1 Municipal and County Courts

4.1.1 Jurisdiction

Ohio has two lower trials courts of limited original jurisdiction. These courts, know as municipal and county, were created by the Ohio legislature in 1953. Prior to the creation of the municipal courts, Ohio had a Justice of the Peace system. This system was eliminated with the creation of the municipal court system.

Municipal courts were established to serve the territory located in the municipal corporation.[73] The *Ohio Revised Code* specifically establishes a municipal court in each of the following municipal corporations:

> Akron, Alliance, Ashland, Ashtabula, Athens, Avon Lake, Barberton, Bedford, Bellefontaine, Bellevue, Berea, Bowling Green, Bryan, Bucyrus, Cambridge, Campbell, Canton, Celina, Chardon, Chesapeake, Chillicothe, Cincinnati, Circleville, Cleveland, Cleveland Heights, Columbus, Conneaut, Coshocton, Cuyahoga Falls, Dayton, Defiance, Delaware, East Cleveland, East Liverpool, Eaton, Elyria, Euclid, Fairborn, Fairfield, Findlay, Fostoria, Franklin, Fremont, Gallipolis, Garfield Heights, Georgetown, Girard, Hamilton, Hillsboro, Huron, Ironton, Jackson, Kenton, Kettering, Lakewood, Lancaster, Lebanon, Lima, Logan, London, Lorain, Lyndhurst, Mansfield, Marietta, Marion, Marysville, Mason, Massillon, Maumee, Medina, Mentor, Miamisburg, Middletown, Mount Gilead, Mount Vernon, Napoleon, New Philadelphia, Newark, Newton Falls, Niles, Norwalk, Oakwood, Oberlin, Oregon, Painesville, Parma, Perrysburg, Port Clinton, Portsmouth, Ravenna, Rocky River, Sandusky, Shaker Heights, Shelby, Sidney, South Euclid, Springfield, Steubenville, Struthers, Sylvania, Tiffin, Toledo, Troy, Upper Sandusky, Urbana, Van Wert, Vandalia, Vermilion, Wadsworth, Wapakoneta, Warren, City of Washington in Fayette County, to be known as Washington Court House, Willoughby, Wilmington, Wooster, Xenia, Youngstown, and Zanesville.[74]

Additionally, the legislature established municipal courts in Batavia located in Clermont County and Lisbon located in Columbiana County.[75]

As a result of the legislature's actions, there are several different configurations of courts in each county. Some counties have a single municipal court whose jurisdiction covers the entire county. For example, in Hamilton County, where Cincinnati is located, there is one court—Hamilton County Municipal Court. If a case that is appropriate for municipal court arises anywhere in

Hamilton County, it will be heard by the Hamilton County Municipal Court. However, if the offense occurs in the city of Cincinnati, a city prosecutor will handle the prosecution. Likewise, if the offense occurs in the county, the county prosecutor is responsible. In other counties, there may be several municipal courts that combine to cover the jurisdiction. That is the situation in Summit County. Summit County has three different municipal courts, specifically, Akron Municipal Court, Barberton Municipal Court, and Cuyahoga Falls Municipal Court. Lastly, the county may have a combination of municipal and county courts. This situation exists in Clermont County. Regardless of the configuration, all of Ohio is within the jurisdiction of either a municipal or county court.

Municipal and county courts are courts of record, having jurisdiction in both law and equity.[76] Since they are both statutorily created, they have no jurisdiction except those powers outlined in the statute. The grant of powers to county and municipal courts is virtually the same. They were created to handle less serious offenses and civil cases where the amount in controversy is not as large as in the Court of Common Pleas. These courts have jurisdiction over misdemeanor and traffic offenses committed within its geographical boundaries. They may also hold initial appearances and preliminary hearings in felony cases. In the civil area, the court can determine cases in which the amount to be recovered does not exceed $15,000.[77] Civil actions such as replevin (the recovery of property), forcible entry and detainer (evictions), judgment debtor examinations (identifying assets to satisfy a judgment), issuance and enforcement of temporary protection orders, public nuisance, and foreclosure are all within the purview of the court.[78] In additional to these powers, the municipal court is also granted the authority to issue process, preserve order, punish contempts, summon and impanel jurors, set aside a verdict, grant a new trial, vacate or modify a judgment and determine bail.[79] The statutes specifically allow the municipal court to determine, preserve, and enforce all rights involved in the action or proceeding necessary or proper for a complete determination of the rights of the parties.[80]

Some municipal courts may have an environmental and/or housing division. Housing divisions were established in the Cleveland and Toledo municipal courts.[81] Franklin County has an environmental division. In addition to the duties of the general division, these special divisions have exclusive jurisdiction over criminal and civil actions to enforce any local codes, ordinances or regulations. These include building, housing, air pollution, sanitation, health, fire, zoning and safety laws that apply to premises used or intended to be used as a place of human habitation.[82] They also have the right to grant temporary restraining orders and temporary and permanent injunctions.[83]

Like the probate judges of the court of common pleas, the municipal judges are vested with the authority to perform marriage ceremonies.[84] They can also take acknowledgment of deeds and other instruments and perform any other duties that are conferred upon judges of the county courts.[85] Administratively, they may adopt, publish, and revise rules for the regulation of practice and procedure for their respective court and for the manner and selection of summoning persons to serve as jurors in the court.[86]

4.1.2 Procedure

Civil actions and proceedings in the municipal court are commenced pursuant to the *Ohio Rules of Civil Procedure*. This procedure is the same as in the Court of Common Pleas. See "Procedure" under Ohio Court of Common Pleas. Appeals from the municipal court may be taken to the appropriate Ohio Court of Appeals.[87] The municipal court clerk is responsible to transmit the record on appeal to the clerk of the appellate court.[88]

Judges

To be eligible for the municipal bench, candidates must be admitted to practice law in the state of Ohio and must have either practiced law in Ohio for at least six years preceding his or her term or served as a judge of a court of record in any jurisdiction in the United States.[89] The voters within the jurisdiction elect all municipal court judges on a nonpartisan ballot for six-year terms.[90] The judges of the housing and environmental divisions are elected specifically to that division.[91] In counties with multiple municipal court judges, elections will be staggered.[92]

The statutes also provide for a presiding judge who is responsible for the general supervision of the business of the court.[93] In counties with only one judge, that judge shall be designated as the presiding judge.[94] In counties with two judges, the judge whose term next expires shall be designated as the presiding judge.[95] In a municipal court having three or more judges, the judges of the court shall select the presiding judge.[96] When the volume of cases pending in any municipal court necessitates an additional judge, the presiding judge can make a written request to the Chief Justice of the Ohio Supreme Court. If granted, the Ohio Supreme Court will designate a judge of another municipal or county court to assist for the necessary time period.[97]

A judge may be removed from office if he or she willfully and flagrantly exercises authority or power not authorized by law, refuses or willfully neglects to enforce the law or to perform any official duty imposed upon him or her by law, or is guilty of gross neglect of duty, gross immorality, drunkenness, misfeasance, malfeasance, or nonfeasance.[98] If a vacancy does occur, the Chief Justice of the Supreme Court may designate a judge of another municipal court to serve until that vacancy is filled.[99] The governor will appoint a qualified candidate to fill the vacancy.[100] If only a temporary vacancy occurs due to absence or incapacitation and the municipal court has only one judge, that municipal judge can appoint a qualified substitute.[101]

4.1.3 Personnel

Every municipal court shall have a clerk that may either be appointed or elected depending on the county and its size.[102] The larger counties will have an elected clerk while the smaller counties will appoint their clerk. In counties where county and municipal courts exist, the clerk of the county court shall also serve as the clerk of the municipal court.[103] In the case of an election, the qualified electors of the territory choose the clerk for a six-year term.[104] The municipal court clerk is responsible to prepare and maintain the court records, issue summons or other process, administer oaths, take affidavits, and issue executions upon judgments.[105] They accept for filing all pleadings except for those by a person who has been found to be a vexatious litigator. A vexatious litigator is any person who has habitually, persistently, and without reasonable grounds engaged in filing civil actions to harass, delay, or maliciously injure another party to the civil action or whose conduct is not warranted under existing law and cannot be supported by a good faith argument for an extension, modification, or reversal of existing law.[106] The clerk is also empowered to accept all fees, fines, bail, and other monies payable to the office.

The municipal court shall also appoint bailiffs, constables, interpreters, mental health professionals, probation officers, and an administrator who serve in the same capacity as their counterparts in the court of common pleas.

The judges of the housing or environment divisions have the authority to appoint a chief housing or environmental specialist and referees.[107]

4.1.4 Small Claims Court

The *Ohio Revised Code* requires the municipal and county courts to have a Small Claims Division.[108] As the name implies, the small claims court is established to handle civil cases where the amount in controversy is relatively small. A plaintiff may present their own claim to avoid legal costs in a relatively inexpensive and simplified forum. The plaintiff is limited to seeking monetary damages only, and the amount demanded cannot exceed $3,000, exclusive of costs and interest. There are several civil actions where the state legislature specifically denied jurisdiction to the small claims court: libel, slander, malicious prosecution, and abuse of process actions.[109] Additionally, the courts cannot grant punitive or exemplary damages.[110] There are no equitable remedies available in small claims court.

There are several advantages to the parties in utilizing the small claims court since the technical legal requirements have been relaxed. The entire process is simplified beginning with the commencement of the action. Unlike the other trial courts that require the filing of a complaint prepared pursuant to the civil rules, actions in small claims court begin with the filing of a simple statement on a court-prepared form.[111] Oftentimes, the court clerk offers assistance in its preparation. The state statutes also reduce the filing fee.[112] The plaintiff cannot request a trial by jury since that right is waived by filing in this division.[113] The clerk will forward the form and summons by certified mail, return receipt requested to the defendant. The defendant should file an answer, if possible. If the defendant files an answer with a counterclaim that exceeds $3,000, the case will be transferred to the regular docket of the municipal or county court.[114] Normally discovery will not take place. A party cannot hold depositions or send interrogatories without receiving permission from the court.[115] The defendant must appear and defend at trial to avoid a default judgment.[116] The trial will be held no less than fifteen days and no more than forty days after the defendant received notice of the action.[117]

Most plaintiffs proceed "**pro se,**" a Latin term meaning they are representing themselves; however they can be represented by counsel. An exception exists if the plaintiff is a corporation.[118] Under those circumstances, an officer or salaried employee of the corporation can present a claim or defense, but only an attorney may engage in cross examination, argument, or other acts of advocacy.[119] As a result, most magistrates encourage corporations to be represented by counsel.

Assuming that the defendant properly receives notification of the plaintiff's claim, the case proceeds to trial. The parties present their evidence to a magistrate. A magistrate is an attorney admitted to the practice of law in Ohio who has been appointed by the court to hear such cases.[120] The rules of evidence do not apply to the proceedings, but the plaintiff still has the burden of proof.[121] In most civil cases, the burden of proof is preponderance of the evidence. The magistrates realize that most parties do not have any legal training and will attempt to assist them in the presentation of their case. After both parties have presented their arguments and evidence, the magistrate will issue a decision.

4.1.5 Mayor's Court

Mayors' courts, established by the *Ohio Revised Code,* are trial courts of limited jurisdiction. As the name implies, the mayor is the presiding judge. The mayor is an elected official and is not required to be a licensed attorney. As a result, the Ohio Supreme Court requires them to complete special legal courses to assist in their decision-making function. However, a recent federal court decision ruled that in some cases a potential conflict of interest existed for mayors to preside over the procedures and render decisions. As a result, magistrates have been appointed by mayors to hear those cases in which a conflict exists.[122] The magistrates are required to be licensed attorneys with at least three years of experience.[123]

Mayors' courts have no civil jurisdiction. They are permitted to hear traffic offenses and some misdemeanor cases that violate the municipal ordinances. They may also punish contempts, compel the attendance of jurors and witnesses, and establish rules for the examination and trial of all cases brought before the court.[124] The police chief or marshal is required to attend the city or village's hearings.[125] The Mayor's court does not have jurisdiction to conduct a trial by jury.[126] If a defendant requests a trial by jury, the case is transferred to the appropriate municipal or county court.[127]

Appeals from the mayor's or magistrate's decisions may be taken to the municipal or county court having jurisdiction within the municipal corporation.[128] A Notice of Appeal that designates the order or judgment appealed from must be filed with the mayor's court within ten days after the mayor's decision.[129] An appeal from the mayor's court to the municipal or county court shall proceed as a **trial de novo.**[130] Trial de novo means that a trial will begin again before the new court. It is as if the previous trial in mayor's court had not occurred. Each side will present their evidence to the new judge in municipal or county court.

CHAPTER 5

5.1 Ohio Court of Common Pleas

5.1.1 Jurisdiction

Article IV, Section 4 of the Ohio Constitution provides that "There shall be a court of common pleas . . . serving each county of the state."[131] As a result, there are eighty-eight courts of common pleas, one per county, being served by one or more judges. The number of judges per county is set by statute and varies based on the court's caseload and the size of the county. These trial courts in the Ohio judicial system have general jurisdiction enabling them to handle virtually any subject matter that occurs within their particular county. Since the Ohio Constitution establishes this jurisdiction, its boundaries cannot be changed without a constitutional amendment. The Court of Common Pleas will hear all "justiciable matters" and review proceedings of administrative officers and agencies as provided by law.[132] They have the authority to determine cases involving both legal and equitable remedies. Legal remedies generally involve monetary damages while equitable remedies are pursued when monetary damages are inadequate. An injunction, an example of an equitable remedy, is an order of the court requiring a party to do something or refrain from doing something. For example, if a factory is dumping large amounts of chemicals into a river, the court may grant an injunction forcing them to stop.

A major category of cases heard by the Court of Common Pleas includes civil matters. These include such actions as negligence, wrongful death, medical malpractice, breach of contract, product liability, and intentional torts. Although technically the court can accept a civil case where the amount in controversy is $500 or more, as a practical matter, a monetary limitation has been placed on civil cases that can be filed in this court. The current amount in controversy should exceed $15,000 before the Court of Common Pleas will exercise jurisdiction.

Criminal cases constitute another major category of Court of Common Pleas cases. They have the power to decide felony cases after an indictment or information has been returned. Felonies are crimes where the possibility of imprisonment may be for one year or more. In Ohio, the accused felon makes an Initial Appearance and may attend a preliminary hearing in the lower trial court, known as municipal court. At the Initial Appearance, the judge will advise the defendant of the charge and evaluate whether bail is appropriate. The next step is the preliminary hearing where the judge will determine the existence of probable cause. Assuming that probable cause is established, the case is bound over to the grand jury for a second evaluation of probable cause. The grand jury can return a true bill if they determine probable cause exists or a no true bill if there is not probable cause. If the grand jury returns a true bill, the defendant is served with an indictment, and the case now proceeds to the Court of Common Pleas. Some counties have adopted a rapid indictment system in which cases are presented to the grand jury without the necessity of a preliminary hearing. The judge of the Court of Common Pleas will schedule an arraignment where once again the defendant will be advised of his rights, the judge will review bail, and the case will be set for trial. If the defendant is found guilty at trial, the judge will order a presentencing investigation that will provide useful information in determining the penalty imposed on the defendant. In summary, the municipal court handles the initial appearance and preliminary hearing; the arraignment, trial, and sentencing are the responsibility of the Court of Common Pleas.

Other areas specifically identified in the *Ohio Revised Code* granting the Court of Common Pleas original jurisdiction are as follows:

- Wrongful imprisonment claims.[133]
- Actions to protect fair housing rights.[134]
- Franklin County Common Pleas only has jurisdiction of any action against the liquor control commission, enforcement agents of the department of public safety, the superintendent of liquor control, or the division of liquor control.[135]
- The extraordinary writs of mandamus[136] and habeas corpus[137]—the court of common pleas has concurrent jurisdiction with the Court of Appeals and Ohio Supreme Court in these areas.
- Injunctions.
- The enforcement of arbitration agreements.[138]
- Applications for an order confirming, vacating, modifying, or correcting an award in an arbitration proceeding.[139]

The Court of Common Pleas has authority to review proceedings of administrative officers and agencies as provided by law, including the following:

- A person aggrieved by a decision of the Board of County Commissioners for locating, establishing, altering, straightening, widening, or changing the direction of a public road.
- A party aggrieved by a final order of the Civil Rights Commission regarding an unlawful discriminatory practice may obtain judicial review.[140]
- A property owner may appeal a decision of the County Board of Revision.[141]
- Appeals from decisions of any agency of any political subdivision.[142]
- In actions for the appropriation of property or any appeal in a road case, in a sewer district case, or in any county water supply system the probate judge may certify the case to the Court of Common Pleas.[143]

The Ohio statutes allow for the Court of Common Pleas to have several divisions that concentrate on one or more areas of the law. Not only do the judges specialize in a particular area, but the results are also generally more consistent. There are four possible divisions in Ohio. They are probate, juvenile, domestic relations, and drug court. In some counties, the common pleas judge may sit as judge in one or more divisions. In the larger counties, the judges decide cases exclusively in their specific division.

5.1.2 *Probate Division*

Every county has a probate division that is empowered to hear matters relating to the administration of estates after the death of an Ohio resident.[144] They can interpret and determine the validity of wills, process and distribute the estate, and appoint executors, administrators, conservators, trustees, and guardians.[145] More recently they have been granted the power to decide complaints that pertain to the status of life-sustaining treatment, nutrition, and hydration in connection with patients in a terminal condition or in a permanently unconscious state.[146] Their jurisdiction also extends over adoptions, name changes, and competency hearings.[147] Additionally, they can issue marriage licenses, and a probate judge may perform marriages.[148]

5.1.3 *Domestic Relations Division*

Another division of the Court of Common Pleas is domestic relations. This division has jurisdiction over all proceedings related to a marriage and its termination.[149] This includes divorce, dissolution, child support, child custody, visitation, spousal support, and division of marital property. They are also vested with the authority to issue an annulment or legal separation.[150]

5.1.4 *Juvenile Division*

The mission of the Juvenile Court as stated in *Ohio Revised Code* Section 2151.01 is to provide for the care, protection, and mental and physical development of children.[151] As a result, the court has broad jurisdiction in dealing with issues involving and related to juveniles. They hear cases with persons under 18 years of age who are charged with traffic offenses and cases dealing with unruly, delinquent, abused, dependent, and neglected children.[152] Delinquency offenses are those in which a juvenile is charged with an offense that would be a criminal charge if the child were an adult. Unruly cases are those in which a juvenile is charged with an offense that is based on that child's status as a juvenile, such as violation of curfew, truancy, and runaway charges. If there is probable cause to believe that a child is mentally ill and should be hospitalized by court order, Juvenile Court will exercise jurisdiction.[153] They also hear adult cases involving paternity, child abuse, contributing to the delinquency of a minor, and all other misdemeanor cases charging adults with acts or omissions with children.[154] If a child is not the issue of a marriage, juvenile court can decide cases involving support, visitation, and custody. A juvenile can petition the court for permission to marry.[155] They can also petition the court for permission for an abortion.

In 2001, the Ohio state legislature responded to the need to provide a safe haven for newborns abandoned by a parent by granting Juvenile Court authority over these cases. Under these statutes a parent, without expressing an intent to return for the child, may voluntarily deliver a newborn less than seventy-two hours old to an emergency medical service worker, peace officer, or hospital employee.[156] Providing that the child has not suffered a physical or mental wound, injury, disability, or condition of a nature that reasonably indicates abuse or neglect of the child, the parent is granted immunity from prosecution.[157] Juvenile Court can issue a temporary custody order to a public children's services agency or a private child-placing agency.[158] The child will be treated as a child adjudicated neglected.[159]

5.1.5 Court-Guided Addiction Treatment Program

In response to the increased number of drug offenses and the corresponding crimes committed to support offender's drug habits, some Courts of Common Pleas have created a Court-Guided Addiction Treatment Program, commonly referred to as Drug Court.[160] Hamilton County began a drug court in March 1995, installing it full-time as part of the Court of Common Pleas in 1996. The Hamilton County program is patterned after national programs geared as an alternate to the traditional courts and adheres to the policy that by providing community-based treatment and judicial monitoring, the recidivism rates would decrease, thereby making communities safer. The target population are arrestees who are drug dependent or in danger of becoming drug dependent. To qualify the defendant must meet the following criteria: (1) the defendant must be charged with a fourth or fifth degree felony; (2) the defendant has no history of violent behavior; (3) the arrest and/or past criminal behavior is drug driven; (4) the Hamilton County Prosecutor must approve of all the incarcerated offender's applications; (5) the defendant must have no active mental illness; and (6) the offender must demonstrate a sincere willingness to participate in a fifteen-month treatment process and have no acute health conditions.[161] As a result of the documented success of the Hamilton County Court-Guided Addiction Treatment Program, other counties are establishing similar programs.

5.1.6 Procedure

A civil case filed in the Ohio Court of Common Pleas is procedurally controlled by the **Rules Governing the Courts of Ohio.** The filing of a complaint with the clerk of courts commences the action.[162] In some cases, like a divorce or dissolution, the complaint is referred to as a petition. A complaint should contain a short and plain statement of the plaintiff's claim and their demand for relief.[163] If a plaintiff seeks more than $25,000, they should state that intention in the pleading.[164] They should not specify the actual amount of recovery they are seeking unless the claim is based upon an account or other written instrument.[165] After proper service of the complaint, the defendant is required to file their responsive pleading to the complaint, referred to as an answer. Normally, the defendant denies the cause of action contained in plaintiff's complaint. The answer may also include affirmative defenses, a counterclaim, or a cross-claim.[166] If the answer includes an affirmative defense, the plaintiff is not required to respond since the court assumes they are denied. However, if the answer contains a counterclaim or cross-claim, the plaintiff must file a response or answer.[167] The only other pleadings recognized by the courts are third-party complaints and the answers thereto.[168] A third-party complaint, filed by the defendant against a third party who is not named in the original complaint, alleges that the third party is liable to the defendant. The third party must then file an answer, which is their response to the allegations contained in the third-party complaint.[169]

Every pleading, motion, or other paper filed with the court must be signed by an attorney of record in the attorney's individual name.[170] They must also include their address and attorney registration number issued by the Ohio Supreme Court.[171] The local rules of each county's Court of Common Pleas may require additional information such as the telephone number with area code. The signature of the attorney on the documents constitutes a certificate by the attorney that they have read the document and that to the best of their belief there are good grounds to support it.[172] If an attorney willfully violates this rule, they can be subjected to appropriate action by the judge. This might include an award to the opposing party of expenses and reasonable attorney fees incurred.[173] Pleadings in Ohio generally do not need to be verified or accompanied by an affidavit.[174] Verification is a sworn statement that the facts contained in the pleading are true. All pleadings and other papers filed with the clerk, including those filed by electronic means, shall be on paper not exceeding 8½ × 11 inches in size without backing or cover.[175]

5.1.7 Judges

In the interests of the fair, impartial, speedy, and sure administration of justice, every county has at least one common pleas judge.[176] Every candidate for the common pleas bench must be an attorney who has practiced law for at least six years or served as a judge of a court of record in any jurisdiction in the United States. Additionally, they must reside in the county and be elected by those voters.[177] They are elected for a six-year term.[178] Any vacancy that may occur due to death, resignation, removal, or retirement prior to the expiration of the term will be filled by a gubernatorial appointment.[179] In counties that require a separate probate, domestic relations, or juvenile court judge, the judges are elected specifically to the division.[180] The judges of the probate division shall be empowered to employ and control the clerks, employees, deputies, and magistrates of the probate division.[181]

In counties having more than one judge, the judges are required to select one to act as presiding judge. If the judges are unable to reach a consensus on who should serve as chief judge, the judge having the longest total service on the Court of Common Pleas shall serve as the presiding judge until a selection can be made by a vote.[182] The Ohio Supreme Court is responsible to determine the duties and exercise of power of the presiding judge.[183] When a common pleas judge is sworn into office, they take an oath "to administer justice without respect to persons and faithfully and impartially to discharge and perform all duties incumbent on him as such judge . . ." The mandatory retirement age is 70.[184] If a judge has voluntarily retired or retired pursuant to the age limitation, the chief justice of the Ohio Supreme Court may assign the judge to active duty as a judge.[185] These judges are commonly referred to as "visiting judges."

5.1.8 *Personnel*

In creating the state judicial system, the 1802 Ohio Constitution provided for the appointment of a Clerk of Courts for each county. The judges of the Court of Common Pleas appointed the clerk to a seven-year term.[186] Under the 1851 Ohio Constitution, the office changed to an elective position for a three-year term.[187] In 1936, the term was extended to four years.[188] The official title is Clerk of the Court of Common Pleas.

The clerk is responsible for various administrative and ministerial duties in conjunction with the court. These include record creation, record maintenance, record reporting, and record retention of the activities of the court. The clerk is also accountable for the receipt and disbursement of all monies paid into the court system. In addition to the court responsibilities, the clerk is also charged with the preparation and maintenance of records for vehicle and watercraft owned by residents of the county.

The clerk's office is divided into two divisions: civil and criminal. The civil division office is responsible for case filings, foreclosures, and certificates of judgment. This division also records notary public commission for those notaries who are residents of the county. Appeals cases to the District Court of Appeals are also handled in this division.

The clerk's criminal division office handles all felony criminal cases. This division reports the disposition of criminal cases to the state of Ohio's central information storage center. Bonds may be posted in the criminal office, and payments may be made for court costs, fines, and restitution.

Other elected officials that are integral to the Court of Common Pleas include the sheriff and the prosecutor. The sheriff is the chief law enforcement officer of the county and has concurrent jurisdiction with municipal and township police. The sheriff also has authority on state highways. In addition to law enforcement duties, the sheriff is the custodian of the county jail. Therefore, the sheriff is responsible for the transportation and safekeeping of anyone held in the jail. The sheriff escorts prisoners to court hearings and remains at the court sessions and is responsible for serving subpoenas, summons, and writs issued by the Court of Common Pleas. The prosecutor is the county's chief representative in court. Whenever there is a complaint or legal controversy, whether civil or criminal, that names the state as a party, the prosecuting attorney represents the state. The prosecuting attorney also provides legal advice to all county officials and county boards.

In addition to the elected officials, the *Ohio Revised Code* allows the Court of Common Pleas to appoint a court interpreter, criminal bailiff, and chief court constable.[189] The statutory responsibilities of the court interpreter are to interpret the testimony of witnesses, translate any writing necessary to be translated in court or in a cause therein, and perform such other services as are required by the court.[190] The criminal bailiff is a deputy sheriff and holds this position at the will of such court.[191] In counties where there are four or more judges of the Court of Common Pleas, the judges shall appoint a chief court constable instead of a criminal bailiff.[192] The chief court constable, in connection with the court constables appointed by the judges, shall supervise the jurors, along with other such duties as the court may require.[193]

In counties having a population in excess of 300,000 as ascertained by the federal census, one or more psychiatrists, psychologists, or other examiners or investigators shall take an oath of office and hold their positions at the will of such judges.[194] In criminal cases, not more than two psychologists or psychiatrists may be required to report concerning the defendant to aid the judge in the disposition of the case.[195] Each psychologist or psychiatrist shall receive a fee to be fixed by the court.

CHAPTER 6

6.1 Court of Claims

6.1.1 Jurisdiction

The Court of Claims, which sits in Franklin County, Ohio, was developed in response to the legislature's actions allowing suits against the state of Ohio. Prior to the 1912 amendment to the Ohio Constitution, the state governmental bodies and officials had governmental or sovereign immunity.[196] This meant that generally one could not be sued when acting in their official capacity, nor could the state be sued for civil damages. However, the state legislature waived this right and permitted such suits with the 1912 Amendment. The theory resulting in this legislation was based on the fact that persons who are injured because of wrongful acts by the state or its officials should not be denied a remedy. Thus, in 1975, the Court of Claims was officially created.[197] The legislative act provided a limited waiver of sovereign immunity; however, it was silent on whether officers and employees were liable. After numerous lawsuits filed against state officials, the legislature acted again. This time they specifically retained immunity for state officers and employees from civil liability, subject to some exceptions. Those exceptions are: (1) activities arising from the operation of a motor vehicle; (2) actions in which the state is a plaintiff; and (3) actions where an officer or employee has acted with malicious purpose, in bad faith, or in a wanton or reckless manner or displayed conduct manifestly outside the scope of employment.[198]

The jurisdiction of the Court of Claims is outlined in the *Ohio Revised Code*. It is the only statutory court that is granted statewide jurisdiction. It provides that this court of record has "exclusive, original jurisdiction in all civil actions against the state permitted by the waiver of immunity" contained in the statute.[199] It also grants the court exclusive jurisdiction over the parties in civil actions that are removed to the Court of Claims.[200] Therefore, the Court of Claims will hear suits against the state and its agencies for personal injury, property damage, breach of contract, and wrongful death, among others. The Civil Division of the court is responsible for these claims.

The statutes also grant the Court of Claims appellate jurisdiction over claims for an award of reparations pursuant to O.R.C.2743.51. In 1976, the state created a division known as the Victims of Crime Compensation program.[201] The purpose of the program is to compensate individuals who suffer personal injuries as the result of a crime. Recoverable damages include verifiable losses such as psychiatric care and counseling, medical expenses, lost wages, lost unemployment benefits, and replacement services. The individual is unable to recoup pain and suffering. In the case of a death, dependants may recover replacement services loss, economic loss, and certain funeral expenses if the death resulted from a homicide. In either case, the maximum amount of recovery is $50,000 per victim per any one incident.

Until 2000, the Court of Claims had original jurisdiction over the crime victim compensation cases. The Attorney General's office would investigate the claim and submit a finding of fact and recommendation to the Court of Claims, who would, in turn, issue a decision. However, commencing in July 2000, the primary responsibility for the claims was transferred to the Attorney General's office, which will now decide the claims. An aggrieved party unhappy with the Attorney General's decision can appeal to the Ohio Court of Claims.

6.1.2 *Procedure*

Civil actions filed against the state of Ohio fall into two categories. The first involves claims of $2,500 or less. The claim is submitted on a complaint form provided by the clerk of courts.[202] The clerk is responsible to forward copies of the complaint to the Attorney General and the state department, board, office, commission, agency, institution, or instrumentality named as defendant by the claimant.[203] The defendant is required to investigate the claim and file an investigation report with the clerk.[204] The claimant then has twenty-one days after receipt of the report to respond.[205] Within forty-two days after mailing the investigation report to the claimant, the clerk of court or a deputy clerk determines the claim administratively.[206] The clerk of courts or deputy clerk, who is appointed by the Ohio Supreme Court, has the same power as a judge of the Court of Claims to regulate all proceedings before him or her.[207] The clerk may, among other things, conduct hearings, require the production of evidence, rule upon motions, determine admissibility and probative value of evidence, require submission of briefs or memorandum, summon and compel attendance of witnesses, including parties, and call and examine them under oath.[208] The formal rules of evidence do not apply in administrative determinations, but all proof must have probative value that would satisfy the court.[209] A claimant in the Court of Claims is not entitled to a trial by jury in a claim against the state; however parties retain their right to jury trial in claims against parties other than the state.[210] In that event, the jury commissioner of the Court of Common Pleas of the county in which the action is to be tried, upon request, must provide a panel of prospective jurors.[211] However, the trial judge or the clerk of courts may order the trial jury to be selected outside the courtroom and the trial judge may set the procedure for the examination of prospective jurors.[212] At the completion of the evidence, the clerk must submit a written decision and include the findings of fact and conclusions of law.[213] The losing party may file a written motion for court review within thirty days of the entry of the clerk's decision.[214] The motion should include the portion of the determination to be reviewed and state the errors complained of with particularity.[215] The movant also needs to include a memorandum that sets forth their argument and supporting legal authorities.[216] Upon review of the file, movant's memorandum, and any memorandum filed by the responding party, the judge of the Court of

Claims shall enter his own judgment.[217] The judge shall confirm or vacate the clerk's order.[218] He may only vacate the clerk's order if he finds that there was a substantial error.[219] The judgment cannot be the subject of further appeal.[220]

In the second category of cases, civil actions in excess of $2,500, the cases are heard and determined by a judge appointed by the Chief Justice of the Ohio Supreme Court. The claimant files a complaint prepared pursuant to the *Ohio Rules of Civil Procedure*. The clerk serves the required parties notice of the commencement of the cause of action. The court will screen the claim to verify that the proper agency is identified, the proper parties have been named, and there are not any demands for punitive damages, attorney's fee, or a request for a jury trial, since they are not permissible. If so, an amended complaint will be ordered. The court will also require the claimant to complete a Statement of Existence of Connected Actions.[221] This will inform the court of any related claims or cases pending in other forums for which there may be sources for collateral recoveries. If such sources exist, the pending Court of Claims action may be stayed until there is a resolution in the connected case. Assuming that the case proceeds, the judge or commissioner will issue a trial order. The trial order contains, among other items, dates for the trial, settlement conference, and discovery cutoffs.[222] The judge will normally order a bifurcated trial on the issues of liability and damages that will serve to expedite matters. Upon the conclusion of the evidence, the judge will issue a written decision. A party dissatisfied with the judgment can appeal the decision to the Tenth District Court of Appeals.[223]

The filing of a Notice of Appeal on the appropriate court form commences an appeal of a reparations decision with the clerk of the Court of Claims.[224] The clerk of the Court of Claims will serve a copy of the Notice of Appeal upon the Attorney General and appellant.[225] It is the responsibility of the Attorney General to file the record with the clerk of the Court of Claims.[226] The appeal to the Court of Claims shall be heard within ninety days of receiving the Notice of Appeal by a panel of commissioners who shall sit in Franklin County, Ohio.[227] Each commissioner shall be an attorney who has been licensed to practice law in Ohio for at least three years prior to appointment and shall serve at the pleasure of the Ohio Supreme Court and under the administrative supervision of the clerk of the Court of Claims.[228] Decisions by the panel of commissioners can be appealed to a judge of the Court of Claims.[229]

CHAPTER 7

7.1 Ohio District Courts of Appeals

7.1.1 Jurisdiction

The primary jurisdiction of the Ohio Court of Appeals, an intermediate appellate court, is to hear appeals from the common pleas, municipal, and county courts. The Court of Appeals has mandatory appellate jurisdiction over judgments or final orders from these trial courts.[230] They may also be required to review final orders or actions of administrative officers or agencies.[231] The Tenth District Court of Appeals in Franklin County hears appeals from the Ohio Court of Claims.

The state is divided into twelve judicial Courts of Appeals districts. Each district has adopted Local Rules of Court pursuant to the *Ohio Revised Code*. The counties included in each district are as follows: [232]

- First District—Hamilton;
- Second District—Champaign, Clark, Darke, Greene, Miami, and Montgomery;
- Third District—Allen, Auglaize, Crawford, Defiance, Hancock, Hardin, Henry, Logan, Marion, Mercer, Paulding, Putnam, Seneca, Shelby, Union, Van Wert, and Wyandot;
- Fourth District—Adams, Athens, Gallin, Highland, Hocking, Jackson, Lawrence, Meigs, Pickaway, Pike, Ross, Scioto, Vinton, and Washington;
- Fifth District—Ashland, Coshocton, Delaware, Fairfield, Guernsey, Holmes, Knox, Licking, Morgan, Morrow, Muskingham, Perry, Richland, Stark, and Tuscarawas;
- Sixth District—Erie, Fulton, Huron, Lucas, Ottawa, Sandusky, Williams, and Wood;
- Seventh District—Belmont, Carroll, Columbiana, Harrison, Jefferson, Mahoning, Monroe, and Noble;
- Eighth District—Cuyahoga;
- Ninth District—Lorain, Medina, Summit, and Wayne;
- Tenth District—Franklin;
- Eleventh District—Ashtabula, Geauga, Lake, Portage, and Trumball;
- Twelfth District—Brown, Butler, Clermont, Clinton, Fayette, Madison, Preble, and Warren.

In addition to its appellate function, the Court of Appeals has original jurisdiction in several instances that are concurrent with the Ohio Supreme Court. These are cases of extraordinary writs. It includes: (1) **quo warranto,** (2) **mandamus,** (3) **habeas corpus,** (4) **prohibition,** and (5) **procedendo.**[233] The Court of Appeals may also exercise original jurisdiction over any case on review as may be necessary to its complete determination.[234]

7.1.2 Composition of Court and Procedure

Each appellate district has at least three judges with the largest districts currently at twelve judges.[235] The number of judges in each district varies depending on several factors, including the court's caseload and the size of the district. However, each case is heard and decided by a three-judge panel.

To qualify as a judge for the Ohio Court of Appeals, the candidate must be an attorney with at least six years experience in the practice of law and a resident of the district.[236] The voters in the respective appellate districts select judges for six-year terms in a nonpartisan election.[237] The elections occur in even-numbered years.[238] There is a chief judge in each district who is elected by his peers for a one-year term. In the event of a vacancy on the bench, the governor of Ohio makes appointments to fill the unexpired term.[239]

To perfect an appeal to the Ohio Court of Appeals, the aggrieved party must file a Notice of Appeal and Docket Statement within thirty days of the entry of the judgment or order appealed, whichever is the later.[240] The case remains in the appellate district where the case originated unless good cause is shown.[241] In other words, if the trial was held in Hamilton County, the appeal would be filed in the First Appellate District. The party is requesting the appellate court to rule that the trial court made a harmful error entitling them to a new trial or a favorable judgment.

Each appellate district has adopted local rules of court that govern the specific procedures for that district and increase the efficiency of the court's operation. The local rules supplement the *Ohio Rules of Appellate Procedure* and address such issues as the length and format of the briefs, the procedure for requesting oral arguments, time allotment, and whether a case should be placed on an accelerated docket. The accelerated calendar is used to expedite the disposition of an appeal that does not involve complex issues. An appeal assigned to the accelerated calendar must generally only involve one or two relatively simple issues. Further limitations placed on accelerated docket appeals vary from district to district.

The Court of Appeals decides the case based on the record, the briefs filed by the parties, and the oral arguments, if any. The record contains the original papers and exhibits filed in the trial court, the transcript of the proceedings, and a certified copy of the docket and journal entries prepared by the clerk of the trial court.[242] The briefs are written by the attorneys and contain the legal arguments and the supporting law regarding whether the trial court made a harmful error during the trial. The attorneys have the option of presenting an oral argument. However, local rules in all districts limit the time for their presentation to fifteen minutes unless good cause is shown. During the oral arguments, the appellate judges may question the attorneys regarding their legal position and the supporting law.

A majority of the court is required to make or render any order, judgment, or decree.[243] They decide the cases based upon prior Ohio Supreme Court cases, when available. If the Ohio Supreme Court has not addressed the issue, they may rely upon previous Ohio appellate court decisions or use other states'

Diagram 3 Ohio Courts of Appeals Appellate Districts

decisions for guidance. Currently, civil cases take approximately eleven months from filing the Notice of Appeal to argument, while criminal cases take about nine months. Once a case is submitted after argument, it takes an average of thirty to sixty days for a decision to be released.

The Court of Appeals has the option to affirm, modify, or reverse judgments or final orders of the trial courts. All decisions of the Court of Appeals are posted to the Ohio Supreme Court Web site; however only a representative selection are designated for print publication. If an opinion meets any of the following criteria, it can be designated for print:

- Construes, applies, or clarifies recently enacted statutory law or administrative rules;
- Explains, modifies, criticizes, or overrules an existing rule of law;
- Applies a rule of law to facts significantly different from those in previously published decisions;
- Otherwise contributes significantly to the development of the law.

7.1.3 Personnel

According to Ohio law, the county clerk of courts also serves as the appellate clerk of courts in each respective county. They are responsible for the filing and maintaining of all Notices of Appeals and original actions. Other court personnel may include staff attorneys, law clerks, and/or paralegals that perform legal research and may assist in the writing of judicial opinions. There is a court administrator who is responsible for all general office administration including budgeting, purchasing, and supervising nonjudicial personnel. Each district may have a bailiff who maintains order and dignity in the courtroom while the court is in session.

CHAPTER 8

8.1 Ohio Supreme Court

8.1.1 History and Composition of the Court

In 1802, the Ohio Constitution established the first Supreme Court in the state of Ohio.[244] The original court consisted of three judges who were appointed by General Assembly.[245] They were required to hold court in each county every year, so they rode horseback from county to county. The term **"riding the circuit"** developed from this practice. Today, the Ohio Supreme Court consists of seven members and sits in the capital at Columbus, Ohio.[246] Although most oral arguments before the Ohio Supreme Court are heard in Columbus, approximately twice per year the Ohio Supreme Court travels to hear arguments off-site in other Ohio counties in a modern day version of "riding the circuit." Local students are invited to attend the sessions.

The members of the Ohio Supreme Court are no longer called judges but are referred to as "justices."[247] There is a Chief Justice and six justices.[248] The justices technically run on a statewide, nonpartisan ballot, since party affiliations are not listed on the ballot. However, the political parties play a major role in selecting the candidates. They nominate the candidates through partisan primary elections, and once selected, the parties endorse the candidates. The voters of the state of Ohio elect the Chief Justice and the associate justices to six-year terms by popular vote.[249] To be eligible for the Ohio Supreme Court, the candidate must be an attorney with at least six years experience in the practice of law who has not attained the age of seventy years at the time he shall assume office.[250] The elections are staggered so that usually two justices are elected in even-numbered years.[251] However, when the Chief Justice is required to run for re-election, three justices may be elected. In the event that a vacancy occurs between elections, the governor of Ohio has the power to appoint a qualified candidate for the unexpired term.[252]

8.1.2 Basic Jurisdiction

The Ohio Supreme Court is the court of last resort in the state of Ohio. The majority of cases that are filed in Ohio Supreme Court are civil and criminal appeals from the Ohio Court of Appeals that fall under the court's discretionary appellate jurisdiction. For the Court to review one of these cases, it must determine that the case is "of public or great general interest."[253] It will direct the Court of Appeals to "certify the record" to the Ohio Supreme Court.

The Ohio Supreme Court has mandatory appellate jurisdiction in several instances.[254] They must hear an appeal if:

- The case involves a question that arises under the Ohio Constitution or the United States Constitution;
- There have been conflicting opinions on the same question from two or more Courts of Appeals;
- The case originated in the Courts of Appeals (quo warranto, mandamus, habeas corpus, prohibition, or procedendo);
- It is an appeal from the Board of Tax Appeals and the Public Utilities Commission; or
- The death penalty has been imposed.

In addition to its appellate function, the Ohio Supreme Court has original jurisdiction to issue extraordinary remedies.[255] These writs include: (1) quo warranto—to stop a person or entity from doing something when it is alleged that they do not have the legal authority, (2) mandamus—ordering a public official to perform an official act, (3) habeas corpus—challenging whether an imprisonment or detention is lawful, (4) prohibition—to stop a lower court from a particular proceeding that is abusing or usurping their judicial function, and (5) procedendo—ordering a court to proceed to judgment in a case.

8.1.3 Extraordinary Jurisdiction and Powers

The Ohio Supreme Court has the authority to regulate lawyers' admission to the practice of law, the discipline of attorneys, and all other matters relating to the practice of law.[256] To assist the attorney, the Ohio Supreme Court has issued *Supreme Court Rules for the Government of the Bar.* These rules include the requirements to be admitted to the bar including information about the bar examination, attorney discipline, unlawful practice of law procedures and discipline, and continuing legal education requirements.[257] These rules require that every licensed attorney who actively practices law in the state of Ohio must be registered with the Ohio Supreme Court.[258] Once registered, the Ohio Supreme Court issues an attorney identification number. In many counties, the attorney is required to include the attorney identification number on pleadings.

The Ohio Constitution grants the Ohio Supreme Court the power to promulgate rules regarding the practice and procedure in all state courts.[259] The rules become effective unless both houses of the General Assembly reject them. The Ohio Supreme Court is responsible to proscribe rules that set the minimum standards for court administration.[260] These rules, known as the *Rules of Superintendence for the Courts of Ohio,* do not have to be approved by the General Assembly to become effective.

8.1.4 Appellate Procedure

If an appellant elects to appeal a decision to the Ohio Supreme Court, they must file a Notice of Appeal and Memorandum in Support of Jurisdiction.[261]

This must be completed within forty-five days from the entry of the judgment being appealed.[262]

Once the Ohio Supreme Court has accepted the appeal, the parties are required to timely submit briefs identifying the case's legal issues with arguments and law in support.[263] In most cases, the Court will then hear oral arguments presented by both parties.[264] Except for death penalty cases, the parties are limited to fifteen minutes to convince the Court of their position and respond to any questions.[265] In death penalty cases, each side is allotted thirty minutes.[266] The Court may vary the time for oral arguments, either on its own or by motion for good cause filed by a party.

It is the responsibility of the Ohio Supreme Court to determine whether the law has been correctly applied. After the Court has reviewed an appeal, it may affirm, modify, or reverse the judgment.[267] A majority of the Court is necessary to render a judgment.[268] Since the Supreme Court is the highest court in Ohio concerning interpretation of its laws, the only other possible avenue of appeal the appellant has is to the United States Supreme Court. Appeals to the U.S. Supreme Court are not frequently granted.

The Ohio Constitution requires the Ohio Supreme Court to promptly publish its decisions and to include the supporting reasons.[269] The decisions are reported in the *Ohio Official Reports* and posted on the Ohio Supreme Court's Web site.[270] In 2003, the Ohio Supreme Court heard a total of 2,237 cases.[271]

8.1.5 *Personnel*

When one refers to the "court," they are generally referring to the justices collectively. However, there are many individuals who contribute to the court's work. Some of the various court officers include the Clerk, Reporter of Decisions, staff attorneys, law librarian, and the court's administrative director.[272]

The first contact an appellate will have with the court is usually with the Clerk of Courts. The clerk's office is responsible to receive filings by the parties and maintain the official record.[273]

The Reporter of Decisions, established by the Court in 1823 is one of the oldest departments of the Ohio Supreme Court. The Reporter is responsible to publish, or "report," the Ohio Supreme Court's opinions, decisions of the appellate courts, selected trial court opinions, entries, miscellaneous orders, and rule amendments.[274]

There are also staff attorneys assigned to the Court who are often experienced attorneys. Their primary responsibility is to assist with legal research and writing.

The law librarian, officially known as the Marshal and Law Librarian, is another crucial component of the Court. It is the responsibility of the law librarian to organize, maintain, and update the collection to provide the best professional law library for the Court. Although the law library's primary objective is support for the justices and staff members of the Ohio Supreme Court, it is also open to other governmental agencies, attorneys, and the public.[275]

The Court administrative director assists the Chief Justice on a variety of matters including administering and managing the court's daily operations, case management, budget, and personnel.[276]

CHAPTER 9

9.1 Alternate Dispute Resolution

9.1.1 Introduction

Ohio's court dockets are very crowded and litigation is costly. It is not unusual for years to pass before there is a resolution to a claim. To address these problems, the Ohio statutes and the *Rules of Superintendence for the Courts of Ohio* permit the courts of common pleas, municipal, and county to adopt a plan for arbitration of civil cases.[277]

Arbitration is one of two alternate ways to resolve a dispute without using formal adjudication. The other method is **mediation.** Collectively, these methods are referred to as **alternate dispute resolution.** In mediation, a neutral third party, referred to as a mediator, facilitates a mutual resolution of the dispute but has no authority to render a decision. The parties work informally, with the mediator's assistance, toward their own agreement. Cases may be referred to mediation by the court or upon the request of the parties. Mediation sessions are confidential pursuant to Ohio law since it is a nonjudicial form of dispute resolution.[278] Since the results are not a matter of public record, parties often prefer mediation. Arbitration is when both parties agree to submit their contested dispute to a neutral third person or panel to decide their dispute. Arbitration is similar to a court hearing—with witnesses called and evidence taken, although the rules of evidence may be relaxed. Outcomes in arbitration that require parties to comply with the decision of the arbitrator are referred to as **binding arbitration.** Decisions that are not legally binding are known as **nonbinding.** In nonbinding cases, the dispute is transferred back to the court for resolution.

9.1.2 Arbitration

Most civil actions are eligible for referral to arbitration. Ohio law specifically allows medical malpractice actions to be referred to an arbitration board.[279] If the parties agree to submit to arbitration, the decision of the board is nonbinding. The board's decision and its opinion together with any concurring or dissenting opinions are not admissible into evidence if a subsequent civil trial becomes necessary.[280] However, since the results from arbitration are often comparable to trial verdicts, many claimants do not pursue adjudication after arbitration.

Many Ohio Courts of Common Pleas have adopted local rules that govern arbitration. The local rules establish what type of cases can be arbitrated including the amount in controversy, location and time periods for hearings, effect of the decision, and who is eligible to serve as an arbitrator. However, since the local courts adopt the rules, the requirements vary from county to county. Most counties require arbitrators to be members of the bar licensed to practice in Ohio and to have completed specific training requirements. However, arbitration agreements executed between the parties can provide for an arbitrator. Many times, in business contracts, the parties include a clause outlining the terms of arbitration if a dispute arises. If the agreement between the parties is silent regarding the arbitrator, the court will appoint an arbitrator pursuant to Ohio law.[281]

9.1.3 *Family Court Mediators*

The Ohio Supreme Court has established specific guidelines for the use and qualification of mediators in family court. The *Rules of Superintendence for the Courts of Ohio* encourage each division of the Court of Common Pleas having jurisdiction to determine the allocation of parental rights and responsibilities for the care of or visitation with minor children to adopt a plan for mediation of such disputes for the care, custody, and visitation issues.

The rules require mediators who mediate parenting responsibilities to have met certain minimum requirements. They are: (1) a bachelor's degree or equivalent education; (2) two years of professional experience with families, and (3) completion of a basic twelve-hour mediation course (or equivalent experience) followed by a forty-hour, specialized family or divorce mediation training certified by the Ohio Supreme Court.[282] Local courts may additionally require observation of and mentoring with experienced mediators, continuing education, and malpractice insurance coverage. The mediators encourage full disclosure during the mediation process. As a result, mediators may not be called as a witness in a subsequent court case.

9.1.4 *Collaborative Family Law*

A new model that utilizes alternate dispute resolution in divorce, separation, or other family law issues is called Collaborative Family Law. Husbands and wives agree to resolve their differences with minimal conflict in order to reach a mutually agreed-upon settlement. If successful, they eliminate court-imposed resolutions that often do not suit their needs or desires. Each party must commit to the process and acknowledge that it is in everyone's best interest. Unlike adjudication, this process is successful only if the parties agree to cooperate and be completely honest. Counsel represents their client throughout the negotiations; however, parties are more involved in the solution-making process than in typical litigation. The parties and attorneys are required to sign a participation agreement stating that the attorney shall withdraw if negotiations are not successful and the case must proceed to litigation.

CHAPTER 10

10.1 Legal Research

10.1.1 Introduction

Legal research is an essential skill required of attorneys and paralegals involved in every area of the law. An effective attorney or paralegal cannot proceed with a client's claim until they know the current status of the relevant law. Finding the law requires an understanding of the nature of the different resources, how to find it, and verification of its status.

There are two sources of law—primary and secondary. Additionally there are tools that aid the researcher in finding the primary and secondary sources. **Primary sources** of law contain the text of the original law and include constitutions, statutes, administrative regulations, and case law. Primary sources may be either **mandatory** or **persuasive.** Mandatory authority is authority that a court is required to follow. Lower courts within a jurisdiction must follow the decisions of the highest court of the same jurisdiction, as well as the provisions of the constitution and the laws passed by the legislature and its agencies. This is distinguished from persuasive authority, which is law or reasoning presented to a court that they might choose to accept or reject. When that primary law or decision from the highest court from one's jurisdiction is now applied to a situation in a court of another jurisdiction, its status changes from mandatory to persuasive authority. When conducting legal research, the first objective is to find mandatory primary sources. If unsuccessful, a search should then focus on persuasive primary authorities. However, it is important to note that only decisions from courts of other jurisdictions are permitted as persuasive authority since statutes from other states are never considered persuasive. If attempts to find primary authority fail or you have limited knowledge of the topic, the search should turn to **secondary resources.** Secondary sources of law are other types of law books that are not primary but explain and comment on the law. They include writings by other attorneys in the form of treatises or law review articles, legal periodicals, bar association journal articles, dictionaries, and legal encyclopedias. To assist the researcher in locating primary and secondary authorities, there are **finding tools.** Finding tools consist of such books as digests, citations, and indexes to periodicals and are never cited in support of a position.

Constitutions and statutes are compiled in sets of books referred to as statute books or **codes.** Ohio statutes and the Ohio Constitution are contained in the *Ohio Revised Code.* These books are **codified,** meaning that they are published and arranged in a classified order by subject. Court opinions or case law are published in sets referred to as **court reports** or **reporters.** There are several sets of court reports in Ohio that contain the opinions of the different courts. Many states only publish select decisions of the appellate courts; however, in addition to appellate decisions, Ohio publishes some trial court decisions. Ohio has always published some "**unreported decisions**" which are decisions that were not designated to be officially published but have been published in a separate set of reports. Special rules are required when citing to unreported decisions to support a position of law, that is, a copy of the unreported decision must be attached to the motion or brief. However, since the amendments to the *Supreme Court Rules for the Reporting of Opinions* dictate that all Court's of Appeals decisions will be published in electronic format on the Ohio Supreme Court's Web site, the designation "unreported" will no longer be needed or used.

Once the applicable law has been found, it must be correctly cited. **Citations** are references to the authority where the law can be found. **The Bluebook: A Uniform System of Citation** was nationally recognized for many years as the only method for citing authorities. However, in recent years, many legal writers adopted the system contained in **The ALWD Citation Manual.** With the advent of online and disk-based law collections, many attorneys are using these as their primary research tools. The providers of these services are advocating for a change to the traditional form of citation to eliminate preference for a particular publisher. Their position is that one publisher's print volume, which may be at least one year old by the time it is published, is no longer the best reference. As a result, the American Bar Association approved a resolution in 1996 recommending that the courts adopt a uniform public domain citation system "equally effective for printed case reports and for case reports electronically published on computer disks or network services." The American Association of Law Libraries has also supported a "vendor and media neutral" citation system. Many states, including Ohio, have responded to this desire to have a uniform system without reference to a particular publisher. Ohio originally adopted its own statewide uniform system of citation in 1985. In 1991, West Publishing Company became the publisher of the *Ohio Official Reports.* As a result, several changes, including the use of parallel citations and pinpoint page citations, were incorporated into the manual to make it more consistent with those used in West's other publications. **Parallel citations** are citations to the same case found in two or more different reports. Ohio Supreme Court decisions can currently be found in both the *Ohio State Reports* and the *North Eastern Reporter.* The citation of the case in both sources constitutes parallel citations. The current interim version, the **Ohio Manual for Citations (1992)** and **Revisions to the Manual of Citations (2002),** guide the legal researcher to correct citation methods for Ohio documents. The *Ohio Manual for Citations* and *Revisions to the Manual of Citations* are posted on the Reporter of Decisions page of the Ohio Supreme Court's Web site at: **www.sconet.state.oh.us/ROD**. The endnotes in this text are cited according to the *Ohio Manual for Citations.*

10.1.2 Ohio Constitution

The Ohio Constitution can be found in the *Ohio Revised Code* and is the highest primary legal authority for the state. It is divided into eighteen articles, each addressing a different topic. For example, Article IV is dedicated to the judiciary. In addition to the current text, each section contains a notation as to when the text was adopted or amended and a citation to comparable legislation. The state of Ohio does not publish its own official version of the code as some states do. The Ohio Constitution is properly cited as Section 2(B)(1)(g), Article IV, Constitution or Ohio Constitution.

10.1.3 Ohio Statutes

The Ohio statutes can be found in two different formats, the session laws, and the more frequently used form—the code. The *Ohio Revised Code* replaced the *General Code* on October 1, 1953. Like the constitution, the statutes can be found in print in either *Page's Ohio Revised Code Annotated* (published by Anderson, which was recently acquired by LEXIS) or *Baldwin's Ohio Revised Code Annotated* (a West publication). If researching electronically, there are several options; however, some require a subscription or membership. One option is Westlaw, the online version of Baldwin's, where the statutes can be found at OH-ST-ANN. Another option is LEXIS, the online version of Page's. When using LEXIS, the statutes can be found at OHIO;OHCODE. Other options include VersusLaw, which contains selected state statutes, Loislaw, and state of Ohio Web sites, including the Ohio Supreme Court's Web site. Each publisher offers different features including methods of searching and updating procedures. It is important that the researcher is familiar with the different characteristics of each option to ensure that they are citing up-to-date law.

The code contains the public laws of a general nature divided into titles or subjects, chapters, and sections. Following each section there may be historical notes showing the source and the current adoption date, comparable legislation in the federal statutes and other states, and **annotations.** Annotations are interpretations or summaries of the statute through discussions, citations to cases, law review articles, or legal encyclopedias. The statutes can be found through the use of indexes if using print books. Electronic methods may require a search to be composed, while others have no search options available. In this situation, the researcher must already know the citation they are searching. Once the statute is located, it is essential to check the supplementation to verify whether the statute is still current law. Supplementation in published books is often completed through **pocket parts.** Pocket parts, located in either the front or back of the hardbound volumes of the code, contain new material not found in the hardbound volume. Once the hardbound volume is reprinted, the material contained in the pocket part is incorporated into the hardbound volume. Online services normally update the main text without utilizing any form of a pocket part. They may be kept current within just a few days; however, this can be verified by checking the date on the document.

Ohio statutes can also be found in the **session laws.** All laws passed during each session of the Ohio General Assembly are published in chronological order by bill number, not by subject matter. Therefore, when searching for a session law, you must first find both the year of the legislative session and the number of the bill. The session law volumes contain subject indexes that are helpful if you know the general time period when the bill was passed. Session laws can be found in three different sources: (1) *State of Ohio: Legislative Acts Passed and Joint Resolutions Adopted,* cited as Ohio Laws; (2) *Page's Ohio Legislative Bulletin* (Anderson) cited as Ohio Legis. Bull; or (3) *Baldwin's Ohio Legislative Service* (Banks-Baldwin), cited as Ohio Legis. Serv. The preference is to cite to Ohio Laws.

When citing to the statute, the *Revisions to the Manual of Citations* states that it shall be abbreviated as R.C., eliminating any reference to a particular publisher. A proper citation would be as follows: R.C. 2743.03. However, many lawyers commonly cite to them as O.R.C. or simply ORC, unless submitting an appellate brief.

10.1.4 Ohio Case Law

Introduction

After reviewing a case, a court issues an opinion or decision stating the reasons for their conclusion. This is known as **case law.** Ohio case law can be found in several different print publications and online reporters; however, not all court opinions are published. **Court reports** are published judicial decisions arranged according to some criteria, usually by a particular court and period of time. All reported Ohio judicial opinions, including Supreme Court, Court of Appeals, and trial courts, are officially published in *Ohio Official Reports.* However, each one is cited differently, as noted following. These opinions can also be found in the National Reporter System, a West publication. The National Reporter System divides the country into seven regions and includes decisions from the various states in a set of reporters. Ohio decisions can be found in the *North Eastern Reporter,* along with decisions from the states of Illinois, Indiana, Massachusetts, and New York.

These reported decisions are significant in legal research due to the doctrine of **stare decisis.** This doctrine states that when a court issues a principal of law that applies to a particular set of facts the court will follow that same principal and apply it in future cases where the facts are substantially the same. In other words, current cases are decided on the basis of these precedents.

There are several components to a decision depending on the publisher and source. Every case has a caption that includes the name or title, case number, and date of the decision. The name or title is generally the name of the parties involved in the litigation, for example, *Smith v. Jones.* Smith is the plaintiff, and Jones is the defendant. Regardless of who appeals the judgment, the order of the names remains the same, so even on appeal the case will always be titled *Smith v. Jones.* Each case is assigned a case number or docket number by the clerk of courts when it is filed. Following the case number is the date the decision was rendered. Many decisions include an introductory statement added by the publisher—a short explanation of the facts and the nature of the case, disposition and name of the lower court, and whether the appellate court affirmed or reversed the lower court. The publishers also usually include **headnotes** or **syllabi.** These are brief summaries on the various points of law contained in the opinion. Since different editors prepare them, the headnotes will vary depending on the resource. West publishers use a key note system for each topic which can be used to locate cases on the same point of law in other resources. The next major component is the opinion of the court with an explanation of the court's decision. If there is a **concurring opinion,** an opinion of a judge who agrees with the conclusion of the majority of the court but disagrees with the reasoning, it will follow the opinion. A **dissenting opinion** may follow the concurring. A judge who disagrees with the majority decision of the court writes a dissenting opinion. The final component is the disposition of the case by the court, that is, affirm or reverse.

Printed volumes of decisions are often more than one year old when they become available. To allow the researcher access to the most current opinions, the publishers provide **advance sheets** or **slip opinions.** These are paperback pamphlets containing opinions of the court shortly after they are decided, usually one week. Internet versions allow you to check the currency of the database through a feature that displays the inclusive dates of coverage.

Supreme Court Decisions

Ohio Supreme Court cases are found in several different sets of reporters and online services. The preferred source for citing of cases from 1852 to date, according to the *Revisions to the Manual of Citations,* is the *Ohio State Reports,* which is currently in its 3rd series. They are officially published in *Ohio Official Reports*. Cases from 1885 to date can also be found in the unofficial reporter, *North Eastern Reporter*. The Ohio Supreme Court maintains a free Web site on which it posts its opinions from 1972 to present. Effective May 1, 2002, the Ohio Supreme Court's Web site became the repository of all opinions of the Supreme Court, Courts of Appeals, Court of Claims, and selected opinions of the state's trial courts. Searchable databases are offered through LEXIS, Westlaw, VersusLaw, and Loislaw. CD-ROMs by Anderson, West, and the Ohio Bar Association, as well as the OBA's *Casemaker,* are other options. Cases from earlier years can be found in four different sources: 1821–1851 are published in *Ohio Reports;* 1821–1836 are published in *Wilcox's Condensed Reports;* 1831–1834 are published in *Wright;* and 1809–1899 are published in *Ohio Unreported Cases.*

Court of Appeals Decisions

Current Court of Appeals decisions are cited as *Ohio Appellate Reports,* which is now in its 3rd series. They are officially published in the *Ohio Official Reports* and unofficially published in the *North Eastern Reporter*. LEXIS, Westlaw, Loislaw, and VersusLaw offer searchable versions of these appellate decisions. They are also available in CD-ROM format from Anderson, West, and the Ohio Bar Association. The Ohio Bar Association also has an online version, entitled *Casemaker*, accessible to members only. It is limited to cases from 1964 to date. Another subscription-only option is through *Ohio Lawyers Weekly*. Once again, the access is very limited as decisions were published beginning in January 2001. For decisions issued between 1906 and 1923, the *Ohio Courts of Appeals Reports* should be consulted. Unreported Ohio appellate cases are printed in hard copy in Anderson's *Unreported Ohio Appellate Cases* and searchable in LEXIS, Westlaw, and Loislaw. They can also be found in *Casemaker* and the CD-ROM subscriptions. However, the amendments to the *Supreme Court Rules for the Reporting of Opinions* eliminated the controlling/persuasive distinction between unreported Court of Appeals opinions. All Court of Appeals opinions will be published—even if only in the electronic format. Therefore, the designation "unreported" will no longer be needed or used.

Trial Court Decisions

Ohio publishes some trial court decisions, including the Court of Common Pleas and lower courts. If the decisions were rendered after 1962, they can be found in the *Ohio Official Reports;* however, they are cited as *Ohio Miscellaneous* or *Ohio Miscellaneous* 2d, depending on the date of the decision. The full text is also available on LEXIS, Westlaw, and Loislaw, utilizing searchable databases. Some state and law school Internet sites, as well as CD-ROMs published by both Anderson and West, offer coverage of the decisions. The Ohio Supreme Court's Web site also has selected opinions of the state's trial courts.

Citations

When citing reported Ohio cases decided before 2002 under the *Revisions to the Manual of Citations,* the following need to be included: (1) the names of the parties and the *v.* for versus are italicized; (2) the year of the decision follows the names of the parties and is placed within parentheses; (3) a comma follows the parentheses; (4) the full parallel citation is given, beginning with the official citation where available, followed by (where available) *Ohio Law Abstracts, Ohio Opinions, Ohio Bar Reports,* and *Northeastern Reporter*, in that order. However, the *Revisions to the Manual of Citations* has altered this form for decisions after May 1, 2002. First, **pinpoint pages** (a specific page of an opinion) are now given for the official source only instead of each parallel unofficial source. Each opinion posted to the Ohio Supreme Court's Web site will be assigned a "Web cite," that is, 2004-Ohio-1234, making it easier for the user to navigate between the hard copy, print-published version and its electronic version. The date in parentheses of the original citation is omitted because the first four digits of the Web cite, here "2004," would be duplicative. Further guidance with illustrations regarding case citations can be found at the Ohio Supreme Court's Web site: **ftp://ftp.sconet.state.oh.us/RuleAmendments/2002/126600-r.doc**.

10.1.5 Ohio Administrative Law

Regulations passed by Ohio agencies are compiled in the *Ohio Administrative Code,* which is published by Banks-Baldwin. Regulations can be located through several searchable online services, including LEXIS, Westlaw, VersusLaw, and Loislaw, as well as nonsearchable choices offered by the state, such as Anderson's Online Docs.

Administrative regulations are cited as follows: Ohio Adm. Code 109:4-3-09. Note that the word or symbol for section is not inserted after the word "Code."

10.1.6 Court Rules

Both published versions of the *Ohio Revised Code* include annotated court rules, although organized differently. Baldwin's offers the rules in separate volumes, while Page's disperses the rules throughout their volumes. Page's prints the court rules in conjunction with the statutory provisions governing that specific court. Unannotated rules of court are also found in Anderson's *Rules Governing the Courts of Ohio* and West's *Ohio Rules of Court.* Online services, LEXIS, Westlaw, and Loislaw, as well as the Ohio Supreme Court, display the rules. To search the rules in LEXIS use OHIO/OHRULE; in Westlaw use OH-RULES; and in Loislaw select the Ohio Library and then choose the Ohio Code.

Most courts publish local rules. They may be obtained from the court clerk's office or the court's Web sites, if available. The *Rules Governing the Courts of Ohio* and *Ohio Rules of Court* include the appellate district court rules and some Court of Common Pleas court rules.

10.1.7 Secondary Sources

Legal Encyclopedias

Ohio Jurisprudence is a legal encyclopedia, arranged alphabetically by topic. It explains the current status in Ohio of a principle of law. Often, there are references to other secondary resources such as law review articles. *Ohio Jurisprudence* is available in print, CD-ROM, and through Westlaw at OHJUR. It contains Index and Table of Cases volumes at the end of the set; however, the Table of Cases does not contain all Ohio cases, only ones included in the digest.

Law Journal and Law Review Articles

The Ohio Bar Association and each law school prints periodical publications known respectively as law journals and law reviews. The law reviews include articles written by law professors and students, while the law journal may contain articles written by practicing attorneys or judges. These scholarly articles usually discuss or summarize specific legal topics or review legal developments of importance to students and practitioners. Articles often contain citations to statutes or cases. Law review and law journal articles can be found in hard copy or through the use of LEXIS or Westlaw. The search can be for a particular legal topic, by the author or the title of the article.

Legal Treatises

Treatises focus on the law in a particular subject area. They are a narrative discussion that is usually more in depth than a summary contained in a legal encyclopedia and usually include relevant footnote references to other statutes and cases or other legal authorities. Treatises may be found in hornbooks and the Nutshell Series, among other sources.

10.1.8 Aids

Digests

In reporters, cases are reported in chronological order, not by subject matter, thereby making it difficult to locate a case on point. Digests provide an index to reported cases by classifying them by subject matter. They also include a short summary of the court's holding, with citations. Ohio has two digests: Martindale-Hubbards *Ohio Law Digest* and West's *Ohio Digest*. West's *Ohio Digest* has comprehensive Table of Cases and a Defendant/Plaintiff volume to assist the researcher.

Legal Newspapers

The *Ohio Lawyers Weekly* is the leading legal newspaper for Ohio. It contains articles on current legal issues, jury verdict and settlement summaries, proposed and final court rule amendments, and the attorney discipline docket. There are also summaries of judicial opinions from the local federal appellate and trial courts plus the Ohio Supreme Court and Court of Appeals. The Courts of Appeals decisions are posted for one week on the newspaper's Web site, which is accessible for free. The Web site is as follows: **www.ohiolawyersweekly.com**.

Conclusion

Whenever one ventures into the study of law, they can only, at the very best, view a timed snapshot. Since our courts, legislatures, and administrators continually modify the body of law, the study must always continue. The preceding discussion of the Ohio courts provides a historical perspective and a timely examination of the laws of Ohio, but it will always change.

Endnotes

[1]Section 1, Article II, Ohio Constitution
[2]Section 1, Article III, Ohio Constitution
[3]Section 5, Article III, Ohio Constitution
[4]Section 2, Article III, Ohio Constitution
[5]Section 1, Article IV, Ohio Constitution
[6]Section 1, Article XVI, Ohio Constitution
[7]Section 2, Article XVI, Ohio Constitution
[8]Section 1, Article II, Ohio Constitution
[9]Section 1, Article II, Ohio Constitution
[10]Sup.R. 12(A)
[11]Sup.R. 12(B)
[12]Sup.R. 12(C)
[13]Sup.R. 12(D)

[14]R.C. 120.01
[15]R.C. 120.01
[16]R.C. 120.03
[17]R.C. 120.06(A)(1)
[18]R.C. 120.06(A)(3)
[19]R.C. 120.14
[20]R.C. 120.17
[21]R.C. 120.16
[22]R.C. 120.33
[23]Section 5(B), Article IV, Ohio Constitution
[24]Section 5(B), Article IV, Ohio Constitution
[25]Section 5(B), Article IV, Ohio Constitution
[26]Sup.R. 5
[27]Loc.R. 11 of the Court of Common Pleas of Hamilton County, General Division
[28]Section 5(A)(1), Article IV, Ohio Constitution
[29]Sup.R. 1
[30]Traf.R. 1
[31]Traf.R. 1(B)
[32]Traf.R. 1(B)
[33]Evid.R. 101(C)(8)
[34]Evid.R. 101
[35]Evid.R. 102
[36]Evid.R. 493
[37]Evid.R. 501
[38]Juv.R. 1(C)
[39]Juv.R. 1(B)
[40]App.R. 1
[41]App.R. 17
[42]Loc.R. 6 of the First Appellate Judicial District
[43]S.Ct.Prac.R. I(1)
[44]S.Ct.Prac.R. I(1)
[45]S.Ct.Prac.R. XIX
[46]S.Ct.Prac.R. X(2)
[47]Crim.R. 6(D)
[48]Crim.R. 7(A)
[49]Crim.R. 7(A)
[50]Crim.R. 6(A)
[51]Crim.R. 6(F)
[52]Crim.R. 6(G)
[53]Crim.R. 23(B)
[54]Crim.R. 23(B)
[55]Crim.R. 23(B)
[56]Crim.R. 31(A)
[57]Civ.R. 38(A)
[58]Civ.R. 39(A)

[59]Civ.R. 48
[60]R.C. 2313.06
[61]R.C. 1901.25
[62]R.C. 2961.01
[63]R.C. 2313.47
[64]Civ.R. 47(A)
[65]Crim.R. 24
[66]Civ.R. 47(B)
[67]Crim.R. 24(C)
[68]Gov.Jud.R. IV(2)
[69]R.C. 4705.99
[70]Civ.R. 3(C)(4)
[71]Crim.R. 18(B)
[72]Crim.R. 18(B)
[73]R.C. 1901.01
[74]R.C. 1901.01(A)
[75]R.C. 1901.01(B) & (C)
[76]R.C. 1901.13(B)
[77]R.C. 1907.17
[78]R.C. 1901.18
[79]R.C. 1901.13
[80]R.C. 1901.13(B)
[81]R.C. 1907.011
[82]R.C. 1901.181(A)(1)
[83]R.C. 1901.131
[84]R.C. 1901.14(A)(1)
[85]R.C. 1901.14(A)(1)
[86]R.C. 1901.14(A)(2)
[87]R.C. 1901.30(A)
[88]R.C. 1901.30
[89]R.C. 1901.06
[90]R.C. 1901.07(A)
[91]R.C. 1901.051
[92]R.C. 1901.08
[93]R.C. 1901.15
[94]R.C. 1901.09(A)
[95]R.C. 1901.09(B)
[96]R.C. 1901.09(C)
[97]R.C. 1901.10(B)
[98]R.C. 3.07
[99]R.C. 1901.10
[100]R.C. 107.08
[101]R.C. 1901.10(A)(2)
[102]R.C. 1901.31
[103]R.C. 1901.31(A)(1)(e)
[104]R.C. 1901.31(A)

[105]R.C. 1901.31
[106]R.C. 2323.52
[107]R.C. 1901.331(A)(1)
[108]R.C. 1925.01
[109]R.C. 1925.02(A)(2)(a)(i)
[110]R.C. 1925.02(A)(2)(a)(iii)
[111]R.C. 1925.04(B)
[112]R.C. 1925.04
[113]R.C. 1925.04
[114]R.C. 1925.02(2)(B)
[115]R.C. 1925.09
[116]R.C. 1925.02
[117]R.C. 1925.04(B)
[118]R.C. 1925.01(D)
[119]R.C. 1925
[120]R.C. 19501(B)
[121]Evid.R. 101(C)(8)
[122]R.C. 1905.08
[123]R.C. 1905.05
[124]R.C. 1905.28
[125]R.C. 1905.08
[126]R.C. 2938.04
[127]*Brunswick v. Giglio* (1988), 530 NE2d 37
[128]R.C. 1905.22
[129]R.C. 1905.23
[130]R.C. 1905.25
[131]Section 4, Article IV, Ohio Constitution
[132]Section 4(B), Article IV, Ohio Constitution
[133]R.C. 2305.02
[134]R.C. 4112.052
[135]R.C. 4301.31
[136]R.C. 2731.02
[137]R.C. 2725.02
[138]R.C. 2711.03
[139]R.C. 2711.09
[140]R.C. 4112.06
[141]R.C. 5717.05
[142]R.C. 2506.01
[143]R.C. 2101.25
[144]R.C. 2101.01
[145]R.C. 2101.24
[146]R.C. 2101.24(A)(1)
[147]R.C. 2101.24(A)(1)(x)
[148]R.C. 2101.27
[149]R.C. 3105.011
[150]R.C. 3105.03

[151]R.C. 2151.01
[152]R.C. 2151.23
[153]R.C. 2151.23 (A)(4)
[154]R.C. 2151.23 (A)(5)
[155]R.C. 2151.23(A)(10)
[156]R.C. 2151.3515
[157]R.C. 2151.3523
[158]R.C. 2151.2120
[159]R.C. 2151.3522
[160]Loc.R. 35 of the Court of Common Pleas of Hamilton County, General Division
[161]Loc.R. 35 of the Court of Common Pleas of Hamilton County, General Division
[162]Civ.R. 3
[163]Civ.R. 8
[164]Civ.R. 8(1)
[165]Civ.R. 10(D)
[166]Civ.R. 8
[167]Civ.R. 7
[168]Civ.R. 7(A)
[169]Civ.R. 7(A)
[170]Civ.R. 11
[171]Civ.R. 11
[172]Civ.R. 11
[173]Civ.R. 11
[174]Civ.R. 11
[175]Civ.R. 10(E)
[176]Section 4, Article IV, Ohio Constitution
[177]R.C. 2301.01
[178]R.C. 2301.01
[179]Section 13, Article 4, Ohio Constitution
[180]Section 4, Article 4, Ohio Constitution
[181]Section 4, Article 4, Ohio Constitution
[182]Section 4, Article 4, Ohio Constitution
[183]Section 4, Article 4, Ohio Constitution
[184]Section 6, Article 4, Ohio Constitution
[185]Section 6, Article 4, Ohio Constitution
[186]Ohio Constitution of 1802
[187]Ohio Constitution of 1851
[188]R.C. 2302.01
[189]R.C. 2301.12
[190]R.C. 2301.12(A)
[191]R.C. 2301.12(B)
[192]R.C. 2301.12(C)
[193]R.C. 2301.12(C)

[194]R.C. 2301.12(D)
[195]R.C. 2947.06(B)
[196]Ohio Constitution–1912 Amendment
[197]Court of Claims Act, Am.Sub.H.B. No. 800
[198]R.C. 2743.02
[199]R.C. 2743.03(A)(1)
[200]R.C. 2743.03(A)(1)
[201]R.C. 2743.51
[202]C.C.R. 6(A)
[203]C.C.R. 6(A)
[204]C.C.R. 6(A)
[205]C.C.R. 6(A)
[206]C.C.R. 6(B)
[207]C.C.R. 6(C)
[208]C.C.R. 6(C)
[209]C.C.R. 6(E)
[210]R.C. 2743.11
[211]C.C.R. 5(A)
[212]C.C.R. 5(B)
[213]C.C.R. 6(G)
[214]C.C.R. 6(H)(1)
[215]C.C.R. 6(H)(2)
[216]C.C.R. 6(H)(2)
[217]C.C.R. 6(H)(5)
[218]C.C.R. 6(H)(6)
[219]C.C.R. 6(H)(6)
[220]R.C. 2743.10(D)
[221]C.C.R. 15(C)
[222]C.C.R. 7
[223]R.C. 2743.20
[224]C.C.R. 24
[225]C.C.R. 24
[226]C.C.R. 24(4)
[227]R.C. 2743.53(A)
[228]R.C. 2743.54(A)
[229]R.C. 2743.53(B)
[230]R.C. 2501.01
[231]Section 3(B)(2), Article 4, Ohio Constitution
[232]R.C. 2501.01
[233]Section 3(B)(1)(a)–(e), Article IV, Ohio Constitution
[234]Section 3(B)(1)(f), Article IV, Ohio Constitution
[235]Section 3(A), Article IV, Ohio Constitution
[236]R.C. 2501.02
[237]Section 6, Article IV, Ohio Constitution
[238]R.C. 2501.02

[239]Section 13, Article IV, Ohio Constitution
[240]R.C. 2501.05
[241]App.R. 9(A)
[242]App.R. 9(A)
[243]R.C. 2501.07
[244]Section 2, Article III, Ohio Constitution of 1802
[245]Section 2, Article III, Ohio Constitution of 1802
[246]Section 2, Article III, Ohio Constitution
[247]Section 2, Article III, Ohio Constitution, 1968 Amendment
[248]Section 2, Article IV, Ohio Constitution
[249]Section 6(A)(1), Article IV, Ohio Constitution
[250]Section 6, Article IV, Ohio Constitution
[251]R.C. 2503.03
[252]Section 13, Article IV, Ohio Constitution
[253]Section 2(B)(2(e), Article IV, Ohio Constitution
[254]Section 2(B)(2)(a), Article IV, Ohio Constitution
[255]Section 2(B)(1)(a)–(e), Article IV, Ohio Constitution
[256]Section 2(B)(1)(g), Article IV, Ohio Constitution
[257]Gov.Bar R.
[258]Gov.Bar R.
[259]Section 5(B), Article IV, Ohio Constitution
[260]Section 5, Article IV, Ohio Constitution
[261]App.R. 3
[262]App.R. 4(A)
[263]S.Ct.Prac.R. VI
[264]S.Ct.Prac.R. IX(1)
[265]S.Ct.Prac.R. IX(5)
[266]S.Ct.Prac.R. IX(5)
[267]Section 2, Article IV, Ohio Constitution
[268]Section 2(A), Article IV, Ohio Constitution
[269]Section 2(C), Article IV, Ohio Constitution
[270]S.Ct.R.Rep.Op. 1
[271]Ohio Courts Summary–2002
[272]R.C. 2503.05
[273]R.C. 2503.11
[274]R.C. 2503.22
[275]R.C. 2503.27
[276]R.C. 2503.281
[277]C.P.Sup.R. 15
[278]R.C. 2317.023
[279]R.C. 2711.21
[280]R.C. 2711.21
[281]R.C. 2711.04
[282]Sup.R. 16

APPENDIX A

Online Sources

The Internet:

Beginning guides on how to search the Web:
http://www.sc.edu/beaufort/library/bones.html
http://www.lib.berkeley.edu/TeachingLib/Guides/Internet/FindInfo.html
http://www.learnwebskills.com/search/main.html
http://www.tilburguniversity.nl/services/library/instruction/www/onlinecourse/

A Guide to Legal Research in Ohio:

Ohio Legal Research:
http://www.law.csuohio.edu/lawlibrary/stategov.html
How to find an Ohio case:
http://www.udayton.edu/~lawlib/guide7.htm

Fee-Based Methods of Legal Research in Ohio:

http://www.lexisnexis.com
http://www.loislaw.com
http://westlaw.com
http://versuslaw.com
http://www.ohiobar.org/memservcen/maintenance/login.asp

Informational sites:

Ohio Supreme Court Library:
http://www.sconet.state.oh.us/LawLibrary
Ohio State Bar Association:
http://www.ohiobar.org
Ohio Lawyers Weekly:
http://www.ohiolawyersweekly.com
About Ohio State Courts:
http://www.lawresearch.com/v10/state/csohj.htm
About Ohio Legislature:
http://www.legislature.state.oh.us
About the Ohio Senate:
http://www.senate.state.oh.us
About the Ohio House of Representatives:
http://www.house.state.oh.us
About federal courts:
http://www.uscourts.gov

About Congress:
http://thomas.loc.gov
About the United States Senate:
http://senate.gov
About the United States House of Representatives:
http://house.gov
About the United States Supreme Court:
http://www.supremecourtus.gov

Ohio Law (sites containing primary sources):

Ohio Constitution:
http://www.legislature.state.oh.us/constitution.pdf
http://onlinedocs.andersonpublishing.com/oh/lpExt.dll?f=templates&fn=main-h.htm&cp=PORC
Ohio Statutes:
http://onlinedocs.andersonpublishing.com/oh/lpExt.dll?f=templates&fn=main-h.htm&cp=PORC
Ohio Supreme Court Decisions:
http://www.sconet.state.oh.us/ROD/documents
Ohio District Courts of Appeals (contains some opinions but varies by district):
http://www.sconet.state.oh.us/District_Courts
Ohio Rules of Court:
http://www.sconet.state.oh.us/Rules
Ohio Administrative Code:
http://onlinedocs.andersonpublishing.com/oh/lpExt.dll?f=templates&fn=main-h.htm&cp=OAC
Ohio Session Laws:
http://www.legislature.state.oh.us/SessionLaw.cfm
Ohio Code of Professional Responsibility:
http://www.sconet.state.oh.us/Rules/professional
Ohio Court of Claims Rules:
http://www.sconet.state.oh.us/Rules/claims
Ohio Attorney General Advisory Opinions:
http://www.ag.state.oh.us/sections/opinions/ag_opinions.htm

Ohio Citation Guide:

Ohio Manual for Citations:
http://www.sconet.state.oh.us/ROD/pdf/MANCITEmain.pdf
Revisions to the Manual of Citations:
http://www.sconet.state.oh.us/ROD/pdf/Rev_Manual_Cit_02.pdf

Federal Law (sites containing primary sources):

United States Supreme Court Opinions:
http://www.law.cornell/.edu
Opinions from Appellate and District Courts:
http://www.law.emory.edu/FEDCTS
Federal Statutes:
http://www/law.cornell/.edu/uscode

Legal Research Search Engines

All Law—Your Internet Legal Gateway:
http://www.AllLaw.com
LawCrawler:
http://lawcrawler.findlaw.com
Lawgurua:
http://www.lawguru.com/search/lawsearch/html
Meta-index for U.S. legal research:
http://gsulaw.gsu.edu/metaindex

INDEX